THE
SORREL HORSE

THE
SORREL HORSE

Ruth Nulton Moore
Illustrated by James L. Converse

HERALD PRESS
Scottdale, Pennsylvania
Kitchener, Ontario
1982

Library of Congress Cataloging in Publication Data

Moore, Ruth Nulton.
  The sorrel horse.

  Summary: Melissa leaves her housing project in New
York City to spend two weeks on a New Jersey horse farm
where she makes good friends with another girl and with
a horse.
  [1. Country Life — Fiction.   2. Horses — Fiction.
3. Friendship — Fiction]   I. Converse, James, ill.
II. Title.
PZ7.M7878So   [Fic]   82-3136
ISBN 0-8361-3303-X (pbk.)   AACR2

THE SORREL HORSE
Copyright © 1982 by Herald Press, Scottdale, Pa. 15683
  Published simultaneously in Canada by Herald Press,
  Kitchener, Ont. N2G 4M5
Library of Congress Catalog Number: 82-3136
International Standard Book Number: 0-8361-3303-X
Printed in the United States of America
Design: Alice B. Shetler

82 83 84 85 86 87 88 10 9 8 7 6 5 4 3 2 1

To Betty
and the Triple J

Contents

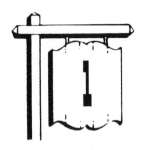

Off to the Country

It was early morning when Melissa and her grandmother arrived at the youth center. A crowd of children and their parents had already gathered on the street corner where two Trailways buses were parked. Everybody seemed to be moving around anxiously, watching the buses, waiting for them to be loaded.

Standing on tiptoe, Melissa looked over the heads of the noisy, excited children around her. Some faces were familiar, for she had seen them in church school. But others were strange. There were black kids and white kids and Puerto Ricans and Chinese. They must have come from all over the East Side of New York City. They wore large name tags around their necks and big, expectant smiles on their faces. Some faces, though, looked anxious and a little frightened—as her own must look, she thought.

As she waited for her turn to get onto one of the buses, Melissa glanced down at her own tag. On it was her name, Melissa Howard, in bold letters along with her address and phone number. At the bottom was printed: Mr. Jeff Mathews, Smithville, R D, New Jersey. And stamped across the tag in big printed letters was East Side Youth Center. Staring at her tag, Melissa felt almost a stranger to herself.

At the sound of her name, her head jerked up, and a strange excitement raced through her. Her grandmother, who was standing by her side, gave her hand a little squeeze. "That's you, Missy. It's time for you to get on the bus."

Melissa felt herself being pushed forward through the crowd as if a big wave were lifting her up to the door of the bus where Pastor Dan stood waiting for her.

She slipped her hand out of her grandmother's. "Good-bye, Gran," she whispered in a choked voice.

"Good-bye, honey." Gran leaned over to give her a kiss. "Be a good girl and have a good time in the country. Say your prayers, and remember that God is always with you and will take care of you." Gran was always saying things like that. There were sudden tears in her eyes, even though she was smiling, and Melissa felt her own heart give a funny twist.

The next thing she knew, Pastor Dan was helping her up the bus steps and was pointing to an empty seat behind the driver. Melissa put her new cardboard suitcase on the rack above her seat. One by one the other children filed into the bus. A girl slid into the seat beside her, but Melissa barely noticed. Pressing her face to the window, she kept waving to Gran.

Gran's eyes weren't misty any longer. She was just smiling now. Melissa smiled back and kept waving until the door of the bus hissed shut, closing out Gran and the familiar sounds and sights of the city.

Melissa felt a strange tightness in her throat as shouts of goodbye rang through the bus, dimmed only by the sound of the motor rumbling to a start. The bus groaned slowly away from the youth center and into the traffic.

Melissa stretched up in her seat to get another look at Gran. But they had turned a corner, and all she could see now were long rows of shabby brownstone buildings and project houses with fire escapes zigzagging up the sides of them. Two boys in front of an empty storefront shouted and waved as the bus rolled by. It seemed as if they were waving good-bye to her forever.

Melissa sat back in her seat. The driver turned another corner, and they crawled down a street filled with taxis and trucks and cars.

They were going across town now. They passed endless rows of apartment buildings and high-rise office buildings, shops, and theatres. Then the crowded streets and tall buildings disappeared as the bus plunged into the darkness of Lincoln Tunnel. When it came out once more into daylight, Melissa had the feeling that she was in another world.

They had left the city behind them and were in New Jersey. Across the Meadows she could make out only the misty skyline of the towers of Manhattan in the distance. Through the golden haze of early morning, it looked like a picture of a magic city she had once seen in a book of fairy tales. It didn't look at all like the city she knew.

Ahead stretched a maze of expressways and turnpikes. Big green signs with strange-sounding names like Weehawken and Secaucus and Passaic drifted by her window. Melissa leaned back in her seat and closed her eyes. She would pretend that this bus was a huge silver dragon that was carrying her to some strange, enchanted land. What would she find there? What would it be like to spend two whole weeks in the country?

Gran had said it would be just fine, just what the doctor had ordered and that Melissa would like the country. That winter a bad cold had developed into pneumonia and had left her pale and thin. Gran worried about her all spring and told Mama that what Melissa needed more than anything else this summer was plenty of fresh air and sunshine. But Mama was too busy with her new job to take a vacation this year. Besides, there was no money even for a weekend trip to the shore.

Then one Sunday Melissa's church-school teacher, Miss Beltz, told the seventh-grade class about the Fresh Air Fund program which sent children from the city to the country so that they could have a vacation away from the noise and heat of crowded city streets. Gran had heard about the Fresh Air Fund program from church and told Melissa's mother about it.

After a long talk with Pastor Dan, Mama asked Melissa, "How would you like to have a nice vacation on a farm in New Jersey, Missy, where there will be plenty of fresh air and sunshine?"

Melissa wasn't sure she wanted to spend two whole weeks alone in the country. Who needed all that fresh air and sunshine? Besides, she had never been away from the city before, and she wasn't all that sure she would like New Jersey. She knew she would miss Mama and Gran and Gran's apartment in the city housing project. She would miss Harriet and Carmen—her best friends, who lived in the next project—and would probably be terribly homesick.

But Gran told her, "It's not just an ordinary farm, honey. Pastor Dan says it's a farm where they raise horses, and the Mathews have asked to have a Fresh Air girl just your age. Pastor Dan knows how crazy you are about horses, Missy, and thought you'd like to go there."

Melissa had to admit that she did like horses—all kinds. She liked the tired, old gray horse that pulled the trash wagon down her street. She liked watching the sleek brown horses that the mounted policemen rode up and down Fifth Avenue. And whenever she found a picture of a horse in a magazine, she'd cut it out and paste it in her scrapbook.

One time she had found a picture of a horse with a light, shiny chestnut coat and a pale gold mane and tail. She had gone to the public library to find out what kind of horse it was, and after having gone through about a dozen books about horses, she had discovered that it was called a sorrel. Melissa had cut out the picture of the sorrel and had pasted it on the last page of her scrapbook. It was her favorite picture, and whenever she looked at it, she would try to imagine what it would be like to ride a horse like that.

When nobody was around, she would lie on her bed with the picture of the sorrel in front of her and imagine herself galloping across a long green field with the wind blowing the sorrel's golden

After looking through about a dozen books on horses, Melissa discovered that a horse with a light, shiny chestnut coat and a pale gold mane and tail is called a sorrel.

Sorrel Horse

mane and tail and tossing its forelock. She could feel the powerful muscles ripple beneath her as they bounded off and away. Off and away across a meadow to the top of a green hill where her sorrel would stand proudly, its neck arched gracefully, its beautiful sleek body silhouetted in the red glow of the sunset.

She would close her eyes in rapture. "Some day I'm going to ride a real horse like that," she would tell herself dreamily. "It will have a beautiful light, bright chestnut coat with white socks and a long white blaze running down its nose. And when it gallops, its golden tail and mane will—they'll float in the wind as if they were flying! Its nose will be soft and satiny when it touches my cheek, and it will make gentle mumbles in my ear like it's talking to me. And its bright eyes will be gentle and loving." Then she would close the scrapbook and sigh blissfully.

Maybe a vacation in the country wouldn't be so bad if there were horses, she had decided. But now alone in this strange bus miles away from home, she wasn't thinking about her sorrel. She was thinking about the far place in the country where she was to spend the next two weeks.

A tight feeling was growing inside her, and the more she thought about the next two weeks, the tighter the feeling grew. When she thought she couldn't stand it any longer, she opened her purse and got out the pictures of her family she had brought along in case she should get homesick.

She spread the pictures out on her lap to look at them. Her own picture had been taken that year in school before she got sick. There was a recent picture of Gran and an old snapshot of Mama and Daddy. They were all smiling at her— Gran's quiet smile, Mama's pretty face, and Daddy's big, broad grin with his broken tooth and his dimples showing.

Her gaze lingered on Daddy's picture. She couldn't remember him; he had gone away when she was a baby. But she had looked at his picture so many times that she felt she had really known him.

One time she had asked Mama why Daddy had left them. She remembered the hurt, bewildered look on Mama's face when she had said that it wasn't because Daddy didn't love them that he had left. It was just that Daddy could never seem to find the right kind of job, and he had felt worthless and sorrowful all the time. Maybe Daddy was tired of beating his fists at closed doors that wouldn't open for him, Mama had told her. Maybe he thought they would be better off living with Gran in her apartment in the city housing project. Maybe that's why he left.

Melissa didn't feel angry or resentful like some kids whose fathers had left them. She kept hoping that some day Daddy would come back so that she could tell him how much she really loved him.

Out of the corner of her eye she saw that the

girl sitting next to her was staring curiously at her pictures. Quickly she put them back into her purse and turned to look out the window. She didn't want anybody asking any foolish questions about Daddy.

They had left the Meadows and the New Jersey suburbs behind them, and now the countryside rolled by like a green and blue kaleidoscope. Everything seemed so dazzlingly bright and unfamiliar that it made Melissa feel giddy. It was as if her whole life now had been turned and shaken like a kaleidoscope into a totally different design.

She was aware that the girl next to her was moving around restlessly in her seat. She felt a sudden nudge. The girl had drawn a candy bar from her pocket and was offering Melissa half of it.

"What's your name?" the girl asked.

Melissa told her.

"Mine's Rosita Gonzales. Where you going?"

"To a farm," Melissa answered, trying to make her voice sound enthusiastic. "It—it's a horse farm."

Rosita took a bite of her candy. "You gotta be kidding!"

The boy across the aisle leaned over in his seat. "A horse farm! Man, that's real cool. Is it like those ranches you see on TV? I didn't know they had ranches in New Jersey."

Before Melissa could reply, Rosita spoke up,

"Horse farms don't turn me on. I'm going to Smithville—back to the same family I visited last year. They're real neat!"

"I bet they don't have a swimming pool," boasted the girl behind them. "The folks I stayed with last summer have one right in the middle of their backyard. We went swimming anytime we wanted to. Even at night, if we wanted to."

"My family don't have no swimming pool," Rosita replied, "but they got a big freezer in the kitchen that's always full of popsicles, and they got a neat color TV. And last summer we went to a drive-in movie and to a lot of swell places. It was real tough!"

"Were you homesick?" Melissa ventured.

"Homesick!" Rosita laughed harshly. "Nah, my old granny I live with couldn't care less if I never came back."

Melissa nibbled her half a candy bar in silence. She felt a little sorry for Rosita, even though the girl didn't seem to care how her grandmother felt about her. Melissa was thankful that Gran didn't feel that way about her.

The bus slowed down and the children stopped talking. Every face was turned to the windows. They had come to a small town half hidden by a grove of maple trees. A white church with a tall pointed spire stood in the middle of the town square. Around it were clustered small white houses, not one right up against the other as in the city but with wide spaces between them and long yards, like green velvet, stretching out in front. It all looked so neat, so orderly, Melissa thought, like a miniature village on a Christmas tree platform.

The bus stopped in front of a house larger than the others with a YMCA sign in the yard. A group of grown-ups and children, smiling and waving, were standing around the sign.

Pastor Dan stood up by the driver, and an expectant hush settled over the bus. "This is our first stop," he announced. "Please listen for your names." He read the names from his clipboard. "Will you please get your suitcases and follow me off the bus?"

Melissa twisted around in her seat to watch the children whose names were called come staggering down the narrow aisle, dragging their heavy suitcases behind them. They filed out the door, and as he called out the names of the Fresh Air host families from the name tags, Pastor Dan put an arm around each child.

Pastor Dan was young and jolly. He seemed more like a big brother than a minister to the young people of his church. Melissa was glad she had been chosen to ride on his bus.

As the names were called, the host fathers and mothers stepped forward eagerly, waving their hands high in the air as they wound through the gathering to look for their young guests.

There was a lot of hugging and calling out: "It's good to see you again!" "My, how you've grown since last year!" "We're going to have a swell time this summer!" Everyone seemed happy to see one another, and as Melissa watched through the window, she wondered what her host family would be like.

When Mama had told her about the Mathews, Melissa hadn't been sure she wanted to live with a strange family for two whole weeks. But Mama kept telling her that it would be all right.

"They have a daughter your age to play with," Gran had added. "You two should get along just fine, honey. Remember, when people try to understand and like one another, it doesn't make any difference where they come from. They have the same good hearts inside. And they're God's beautiful people."

Gran was always saying things like that to make her feel good—things Melissa didn't quite understand. What she did understand was that not all God's people were as loving and as kind as the ones she was watching now from the bus window.

Oh sure, there were people who went around sympathizing with project people and saying they were okay and everything, but they only felt this way as long as the people stayed in their own projects. She had seen "those others," as Gran called them, in school and in neighborhoods where mostly rich kids lived. She knew by the way they looked and by the way they acted what they really thought of her and Mama and Gran.

Melissa hoped the Mathews weren't "those others."

She watched the Fresh Air children walk off with their host families to the line of parked cars by the side of the YMCA building. She watched Pastor Dan wave goodbye to them, then step back into the bus. The door hissed shut behind him, and they were on their way again.

The boy sitting across the aisle was gone, also the girl in the seat behind them. The bus seemed quiet now and empty. Melissa was glad that Rosita was going all the way to Smithville. She would have felt lonely sitting in the half-empty bus with nobody to talk with.

The towns became farther and farther apart. Fields and wooded hills stretched out before them like a strange new world. They had come a long way across New Jersey, and Melissa had a feeling that it wouldn't be much longer now.

Even so, she was surprised when the bus slowed to turn off the highway and there was no town in sight. When Pastor Dan called out her name and announced that she was the only one getting off at this stop, her eyes flew to the window.

She saw just one solitary building alongside the highway with the sign, *Grayson's Store,* hanging in front of it. Underneath this sign was a smaller one, *Bus Stop.* The bus had pulled up just beyond a row of gasoline pumps to where two people were standing, a man wearing a big cowboy hat and a girl about her age. And that was all she saw except the empty countryside. She felt as though her kaleidoscope had been turned and shaken again, shifting the translucent pieces of glass into a crazier design than before.

"The Mathews live two miles this side of Smithville," Pastor Dan was explaining as he reached up for her suitcase. "It's closer for them to meet you here than at the bus station in town."

The next few minutes passed so quickly that Melissa didn't even have a chance to say good-bye to Rosita. As if in a daze she found herself following Pastor Dan off the bus. Standing outside in the bright sunshine, she blinked her eyes in the glare and felt utterly alone. Everything was so dazzlingly bright, so empty. The tight feeling crept back inside her again as she clasped her hands around the handle of her suitcase and stared in silent confusion at the two strangers who were coming toward her.

The man wearing the big cowboy hat seemed friendly enough. He was tall and lanky, with a fringe of gray hair sticking out from under his big hat. He walked with the same easy, rocking gait of the cowboys she had seen on TV, and she wondered whether there were really cowboys in New Jersey.

Her glance flew to the girl, to the long blond hair held back by a blue band, to the generous scattering of freckles across a turned-up nose, and to the blue eyes smiling a welcome that was warm and shy.

The girl took a step forward. "Hi!" And at that moment the flashing pieces of color in Melissa's kaleidoscope came together again, falling into place, and the tight feeling inside her relaxed a little as she stepped off the bus to meet the girl.

Slowly, expectantly, she found herself smiling back.

The Sorrel Horse

The man in the cowboy hat introduced himself as Ed, and the girl by his side was Jan. He assured Melissa that Mr. and Mrs. Mathews were expecting her. Then Pastor Dan put his arm around her shoulder, just as he had done with the other Fresh Air children before he had left them, and gave it a tight squeeze.

"Have a good time in the country, Missy," he said. "I know you and Jan will soon be good friends."

Melissa nodded. "Sure," she said in a voice high-pitched to disguise the cold feeling that was returning, a feeling which came from knowing that in a few seconds Pastor Dan would be reboarding the bus without her. She flashed him a thin smile as he waved goodbye, and the door shut behind him.

Then her eyes searched the green-tinted windows until they found Rosita's face, like a vague shadow, smiling down at her. Rosita waved and Melissa felt a lump in her throat as she waved back. It was as though she were saying good-bye to a very dear friend.

She stood like a wooden statue as she watched the bus start up and continue down the road without her. She watched until it disappeared around a long, sweeping curve. Then Ed reached for her suitcase.

"I reckon it's time we be getting back," he drawled. "Got a pile of chores to do." He tossed the suitcase into the back of an old red pickup truck and motioned for her and Jan to climb into the cab with him.

Out of the corner of her eye Melissa noticed that Jan limped slightly as they walked together to the truck. "I wonder what happened to her," Melissa asked herself as she climbed into the cab next to the girl.

As they went swaying down the winding country road, Melissa forced herself to look out the window. There was nothing left to do now but to make the best of things for the next two weeks. She sat quietly, watching the strange landscape drift by.

So this was the country! There were huge

green meadows with deep meandering streams cutting through them and brown fields with long wavy designs in the freshly plowed ground. The top of a hill was patched with dark evergreens that looked just like the cut trees that were sold on the street corners at Christmas. Honeysuckle wound around fence posts along the way, making the air heavy and sweet, like the perfume the salesladies wore in the department stores in the city.

Melissa took a deep breath of the fragrant air. She would tell Mama and Gran about the Christmas tree woods and the sweet perfumed air when she wrote to them.

Then, it seemed in almost no time, they were turning off the road and into a narrow lane. Ed stopped the pickup, got out, and opened a gate at the entrance to the lane over which hung a big wooden sign with the name TRIPLE J painted on it. Jan wiggled on the edge of the seat and nudged Melissa as she pointed to the name on the gate.

"That's the name of our farm," she said with a touch of pride in her voice. "Daddy had that sign put up when he decided to board and breed horses as well as raise beef cattle."

"Tell her what Triple J means," Ed said, returning to the truck.

Melissa listened attentively as Jan explained. "Triple J stands for the first letter of our names. Dad's name is Jeff, Mom's name is Julie, and my name is Jan. Three J's or triple J."

Ed put the pickup into low gear, and they started up the narrow lane between a hay meadow on one side and a pasture where horses grazed on the other. Melissa stared at the horses.

There was a brown bay, a sandy buckskin, a splotchy Appaloosa, and a pinto all in one pasture. With their tails and manes rippling in the wind and their long necks arched gracefully in grazing, they looked as pretty as a picture.

She felt another nudge, and this time Jan was pointing to a large stone house at the end of the lane. A woman was standing in the dooryard, and a man was coming from a barn across the way. A big black dog came bounding around the corner of the house, barking and leaping up at the truck as it swayed to a stop. Melissa drew back in her seat.

"Be quiet, Frieda!" Ed commanded through the open window.

The dog stopped barking, but her pointed ears stood straight up, and her plume of tail still wagged wildly.

"She's big and noisy but friendly," Ed said, looking fondly at the big dog as he opened the door of the cab. "She loves everybody at the Triple J violently—people and horses alike."

When Melissa stepped down from the truck, Frieda demonstrated this violently affectionate nature by almost knocking her down in an overwhelming welcome.

"Frieda, stay!" ordered Jan. "This is Melissa.

Sit down and shake hands with her."

The big German shepherd sat down obediently. She opened her mouth in what looked like a big grin and lifted her paw. She looked so friendly that Melissa forgot her fear and reached out a hand to take the paw and give it a shake.

Then Mrs. Mathews gave her a warm hug. "Welcome to the Triple J, dear," she said.

Melissa looked up into the woman's bright hazel eyes. They weren't warm and brown like Mama's, but they were kind and smiling just the same. A faint scattering of freckles shone on her fair skin where the sun touched it. Her short hair fluffed lightly in the breeze. She was small and blond, like Jan, but it was plain to see that it was Mr. Mathews who had given Jan her friendly smile.

"Hi!" he said now as he opened the corral gate and grasped her hand in his own.

They started up the walk together, with Mr. Mathews carrying Melissa's suitcase. They entered the house from a side porch, and Jan called gaily over her shoulder, "We always enter by way of the kitchen. Hardly anyone uses the front entrance."

She opened the door for Melissa, and they entered a large, cheerful room with sunlight falling across an oval rug in the center of the floor. By the window was a comfortable-looking Boston rocker, and on the wide windowsills red geraniums made a bright splash of color. It was the biggest kitchen Melissa had ever been in, and almost immediately she looked around for a freezer that might be full of popsicles.

"Follow me. I'll show you your room," Jan said excitedly as she limped toward a stairway off the kitchen.

At the top of the stairs Melissa found herself in a long hall that led past several rooms. The doors to the rooms were open, and she could see that they were all bedrooms. It was difficult to imagine one family having so many rooms all for themselves.

Jan led the way to the guest room at the end of the hall. Melissa stood in the doorway and peered in at the sunny, powderblue walls and the white ruffled curtains at the windows. There was a pink spread on the bed that matched the pink flowers on the skirt of the little dressing table. A colorful braided rug lay on the wide polished floorboards.

Jan leaned against the door. "Cat got your tongue?" she asked, laughing. "You haven't said one word since we arrived home."

Melissa smiled thinly. It was this strange world that had made her silent—the strangeness of the country, the strangeness of these people, the strangeness of this house. Maybe if she forgot everything else and tried to concentrate only on this one room that was to be her own for the next two weeks, she would begin to feel a little more at home. She'd never had a room all to herself before. She and Gran shared the one bed in their apartment while Mama slept in the living room on a hide-a-bed couch.

She ventured over to the dressing table and touched the wild roses in the glass vase. Their petals felt like velvet, and they filled the room with a fresh, sweet scent.

"They're real!" she exclaimed.

Jan sparkled. "Of course they're real. I picked them this morning from our rose arbor. Do you like them?"

"Uh-huh." Melissa bent to smell the soft pink petals. As she did so, her gaze drifted to the open window. There were no tall brick walls here to shut out the view. The whole empty world stretched out to meet the blue of an empty sky.

She moved closer to the window to get a better look. A long green pasture met her eyes, and in the distance there was a woods. A horse was grazing by the fence in the pasture near the house. She stared at it, not believing for a minute what she saw.

It had a light, shiny chestnut coat with white socks and a white blaze running down its nose. Its beautiful sleek body was outlined against the green of the pasture, and its golden tail and mane rippled slightly as the breeze touched them.

For a moment she forgot her loneliness and the fact that she was in a strange new world. She blinked her eyes unbelievingly and just stared at the horse.

It was her sorrel! She was sure of it. It was exactly like the picture of the sorrel horse on the last page of her scrapbook. She whirled around to ask Jan about the horse, but Jan was busy limping about the room and explaining where she could put her things.

"You can hang your dress in this closet and put your other stuff in that chest of drawers in the corner," the girl was telling her.

Melissa reluctantly tore her gaze from the window and walked over to the bed where Mr. Mathews had put her suitcase. She opened it and took out a pair of pink shorts and a white blouse which she carefully laid on the bed. She took out her nightie, socks and underwear, and her swimsuit.

When the clothes were unpacked, Jan frowned down at the empty suitcase. "Didn't you bring any jeans?"

Melissa shook her head. "I brought these to wear," she said, pointing proudly to the pink shorts and white blouse.

Gran had wanted her to look nice during her stay in the country. Gran had scrimped to buy the pink shorts and white blouse for her. Melissa hoped that Jan would notice how new they were.

But Jan ignored the new clothes with a shrug of her shoulders. "Oh, well, you can wear a pair of my jeans. We're about the same size. That's all we ever wear around here."

She limped from the room and in a few

minutes returned with two pairs of jeans and some T-shirts draped over her arm. "Here, put these on now, and I'll stick the others in your drawer."

Melissa got into the borrowed jeans and T-shirt. When she was dressed, she studied her reflection in the dressing-table mirror and saw a tall, skinny girl with long dark hair and wide brown eyes that had always seemed too big for her small, narrow face. It wasn't at all a pretty face, but Gran had told her that it had the look of determination in it—character, Gran called it— and that was something to be proud of.

"Now you look like a country girl," Jan was saying with satisfaction.

Melissa wiggled her toes in her new blue sneakers. Gran had bought the sneakers and blouse and pink shorts to impress the summer family. Gran had thought it best to leave the old jeans and T-shirts at home. And here she was dressed in them anyway, just like Jan. In a way that she couldn't explain to herself the thought struck her funny, and she started to giggle.

Jan giggled too. Then linking her arm through Melissa's she said, "Come on, let's go down for lunch. I'm starved."

The big oval table in the kitchen was set for two, and Melissa was relieved that just she and Jan would be eating lunch together this first day. As they nibbled potato chips and tuna salad sandwiches, Jan chattered on about the fun they would have during the next two weeks, but Melissa only half listened. She was thinking about Gran eating alone today at the little folddown table in their housing project kitchen. Was Gran missing her as much as she was missing Gran? she wondered.

Lost in thoughts of home, Melissa seemed to have forgotten all else until Mrs. Mathews asked her a second time whether she wanted another glass of milk. Then, remembering her manners, she said, "Oh, no, ma'am. No, thank you." She didn't want these strangers to think she didn't know how to act.

"Suppose you call me 'Aunt Julie' and Mr. Mathews 'Uncle Jeff' while you're here," Mrs. Mathews told her, smiling. "That's what Jan's friends call us."

"Yes, ma'am—I mean, Aunt Julie," she replied, venturing a polite smile of her own. In the next breath she murmured, with a shy bob of her head, "Everyone at home calls me Missy."

"Then we'll call you that too," Jan said, jumping up from the table. "Come on, Missy, we'll do the dishes for Mom; then I'll show you around."

"I'll help you with the dishes today," her mother spoke up quickly. "Missy can help tomorrow. I believe right now she'd like to catch her breath and look around the farm by herself."

Jan turned from the sink, regarding her mother with a baffled expression. But Aunt Julie smiled knowingly. "Across the bottom pasture by the side of the house, there's a short trail through the woods that leads to a kill with a lovely little waterfall. Maybe you'd like to hunt for it, Missy."

With a puzzled shake of her head, Melissa asked, "A kill?"

Mrs. Mathews laughed. "That is what we in New Jersey call a stream. It comes from the Dutch who first settled here."

"Oh," Melissa said. Without waiting for Jan to protest further, she got up from the table and quickly let herself out the kitchen door. She was grateful for this time to be alone, to catch her breath as Aunt Julie put it. First she'd see whether the sorrel was still in the pasture by the side of the house. Then she'd look for the stream, or kill, and the waterfall Aunt Julie had told her about.

She hurried over to the fence where she had seen the horse. A wave of disappointment poured over her when she found that it wasn't there. Her eyes searched the pasture, but not a horse was in sight now. She began to wonder whether she had really seen the sorrel after all.

Back in the city she had often daydreamed about beautiful things that she wanted, but never expected, to see. If she concentrated hard enough, she could see them in her mind, and they seemed very real to her. Maybe it was like that now. Maybe she had just imagined seeing the sorrel by the fence.

She slipped through the bars and found herself

35

in a field of grass that stretched out before her like an enormous green sea. There was nothing close-by, nothing that she could touch. Just acres and acres of space and grass.

But there must be an end, she reasoned, and when she looked far enough, she saw the woods and the gate that probably led to the trail.

The next thing she knew she was running, running to get across the pasture, the grass alive under her feet, winged insects buzzing and whirring in confusion all around her. She ran as if through endless space until at last she reached the gate, breathless but grateful for the sheltering woods.

As she started slowly down the trail, she felt like an explorer on his first journey into the unknown. The tall, silent trees closing in around her seemed a little frightening. But as she walked on, she soon became lost in the beauty of this strange new world.

The trees were so tall that the sun, filtering through their thick, interlocking branches, bathed the woods in an emerald glow. Here and there, where the branches parted, bright splotches of light and shadow danced through the green forest.

What was the sorrel horse doing here in the woods? Melissa wondered. She felt an ache deep inside her that she sometimes got when she had seen something truly beautiful.

"It's unreal!" she told herself. "It's as if I were walking through psychedelic lights."

A soft rippling sound lured her on until she found herself by the bank of a stream. The water's murmuring became bubbling laughter as the stream trilled over a ledge of moss-covered rocks into a dark, quiet pool which was bordered with giant ferns. This must be the kill, she thought, and the water falling over the rocks in a white bubbling stream must be Aunt Julie's waterfall.

Melissa sat on a log. The green glade cupped cool, leafy hands around her. The waterfall sang in her ears. A fern bobbing in the breeze touched her arm. She drew back in alarm, then bent over to examine the delicate green leaves. They were as fine as the lace on Gran's best handkerchief.

She sat very still and listened to the strange forest sounds—the breeze sighing through the pines, the whir of insect wings, the droning of bees among the wild flowers, the small voices of countless living creatures hidden in the trees and bushes.

At home, on the busy streets or in the crowded housing project, there was always someone talking or laughing or shouting or arguing. There was always a stereo blaring or a siren wailing. Here were only the waterfall murmuring its thin laughter over the rocks, the wind humming through the trees, and the birds and insects singing tiny songs all around her. It was weird!

Another sound, the sound of leaves rustling nearby, made her sit bolt upright. She blinked her eyes. There, through the trees along the bank of the kill, was a moving shadow!

She drew in her breath and stared as the bushes parted and a creature as beautiful and as graceful as the willow it stood under dropped its head over the pool to drink. Her heart thumped. What was the sorrel horse doing here in the woods? Why was it drinking by the waterfall?

Entranced, she watched the gracefully arched neck, the pointed ears, the golden forelock that touched the surface of the water, and felt an ache deep inside her that she sometimes got when she had seen something truly beautiful.

"Oh-h-h!" She let out a sigh as faint as the wind through the pines.

The horse lifted its head and stared at her with great, gentle eyes. It blew softly through its nose, one ear dropping forward curiously. Then it disappeared through the trees, silently like a shadow, as if it had not been there at all.

Melissa stood up, her legs trembling. Was her vision real? Had the sorrel really been here, drinking by the waterfall? She was still staring in wonder at the silent trees when Jan found her.

Learning to Ride

Jan's voice rang out like a bell in the quiet forest. "Oh, there you are. I didn't see you behind that tree."

Melissa's eyes looked past the girl at the green woods into which the sorrel horse had disappeared, and she said nothing.

Jan sank down on the log next to her and hugged her knees up close to her chin, her eyes following the rush of water to the waterfall. "It's neat here, isn't it? I mean, because it's so cool and quiet and everything."

Melissa nodded. She wanted to ask Jan about the sorrel she had seen drinking by the waterfall. But she didn't trust herself to talk about the beautiful horse. Maybe it was because she wasn't sure the sorrel really existed. The sight of the horse drinking at the kill had seemed so elusive, so very much like one of her dreams. So she sat without speaking, keeping it all to herself.

Jan tossed a leaf into the kill. They watched it drift toward the waterfall, then turn and twist and whirl as it traveled down the white cascade of water. They watched it bob up at the bottom amid the white foam. When it floated away, Jan turned to Melissa, a happy glow on her face.

"I'm so glad you're here, Missy," she said. "With school out, it gets lonesome on the farm in the summer. I suppose in the city there are lots of kids to play with."

"Uh-huh," Melissa murmured, thinking of her two best friends, Harriet and Carmen. What were they doing now? she wondered. Probably having fun on the playground or hanging around the Sweet Shop on the corner, rapping with the other kids. And here she was a million miles away in a lonely woods, talking to a strange girl whose world was so different from her own.

"Of course, Audrey Van Doren comes over sometimes," Jan continued. "Her dad owns those big stables over by the highway. Anyway, she's my best friend and the cutest and most popular girl in the seventh grade."

Melissa sensed Jan's pride in being best friends with the cutest and most popular girl in her class.

"But it's not like having someone here all the

time to have fun with," Jan went on, "so when Dad and Mom heard about the Fresh Air Fund program in New York, they thought it would be neat to have you come."

Melissa dropped her eyes resentfully. *Yeah, all they wanted me for was to keep their precious daughter company for two weeks this summer— and to feel good about doing their duty in getting a poor, unfortunate kid out of the city.*

Well, she thought, this poor, unfortunate kid would rather be back in the city housing project, where she belongs—with Gran and Mama and Harriet and Carmen. Couldn't they see how crazy it was to send her here?

Jan jumped up from the log. "Come on, let's get our swimsuits; then we can come back here and swim in the pool. We can swim all afternoon if you like."

Melissa glanced down at the deep, fern-ringed pool below the waterfall. It was a warm day and the pool did look inviting. As she followed Jan back through the woods, she noticed that Jan's limp was more pronounced along the uneven trail. She couldn't resist asking the question that had hung in the back of her mind since they had first met. "What happened to your leg?"

Jan was silent for a moment, and Melissa thought she wasn't going to answer. Then, the gaiety gone from her voice, she replied, "I fell from a horse when I was six years old. Mom said I was too young to ride, but Dad wanted me to grow up to be a good horsewoman. So he started me early. I was doing all right until the horse started to jog. Then I got scared and wanted to get off. Dad had taught me how to slow down, but I got panicky and fell off."

Jan paused and glanced down at her leg. "I injured it pretty bad, and the doctor said I'd always have a slight limp. Dad told me that wouldn't stop me from being a good rider, but I'll never get back on a horse again."

"Why not?" Melissa asked. She couldn't imagine anyone not wanting to ride, and after all, Jan's accident had happened a long time ago, when she was very young.

Jan's voice and face were sullen. "Because I just won't," she replied, tight-lipped. She swung around and continued down the path, trying her best to disguise the limp.

They walked in silence until they reached the pasture. As they were coming out of the woods, they saw Ed by the pasture gate, leading a horse up to the corral. He turned when he saw them coming and called out, "Nice day for a ride and this little mare is rarin' to go."

Melissa stopped short and caught her breath. The little mare Ed was referring to had a light, shiny chestnut coat with white socks and a long white blaze running down her nose. Her mane and tail were golden, and her shining neck curved downward as she lowered her head to nibble the pasture grass.

Melissa blinked her eyes. She was almost afraid to look at the sorrel for fear that it might disappear again. But it didn't. Instead, it lifted its head and nickered softly at the girls.

"Her name's Shadow, and Jeff picked her out for your horse to ride, Missy," Ed said. "She's a real lady, gentle and patient, and knows her way around the countryside."

Melissa's breath came out in a happy gasp. "Oh, wow! I mean...." And at that moment all she could think of to say was, "She's real!"

"Of course she's real," laughed Ed.

"I mean," Melissa hurried to explain, "I saw a horse—or thought I saw one—just like her a while ago by the waterfall."

"Most likely you left the gate open, and she followed you there," Ed replied. "Shadow will follow anybody anywhere around the farm. That's how she got her name. 'Like me and my shadow,' Jeff used to say, and the name stuck."

Ed ran a hand across the mare's withers. "She's gentle and she'll like you after she gets to know you, Missy. Let's see how she takes sugar off the palm of your hand."

"You—you mean I can feed her?"

"Sure can." Ed reached into his pocket for a sugar cube and showed Melissa how to hold it flat on the palm of her hand so that the horse could take it without nibbling her fingers.

Melissa held out her hand, and the sorrel stepped daintily toward her. The horse's delicate nostrils dilated, and Melissa felt the nose, soft and satiny, touch her palm as, ever so gently, the quivering lips reached for the sugar. At that very moment a surge of joy swept through Melissa, a joy she had never known before. She reached out to run her hand down the long muzzle, and the sorrel quivered at her touch.

"There! What did I tell you?" Ed drawled with satisfaction. "She's taken a fancy to you right off. Now let's mosey up to the tack room and get a saddle. If you want to ride her, you've got to learn how."

Jan hung back. "But, Ed, we were going swimming," she protested.

The man turned as if he hadn't heard her.

"Missy doesn't know or care anything about horses! Do you, Missy?" Jan continued, her blue eyes looking pleadingly at the city girl.

But Melissa wasn't listening to Jan's plea. It was as if nothing else existed around her at that moment except the beautiful sorrel horse. As if in a daze she followed Shadow across the meadow and up the lane that led to the barn.

After closing the big wooden gate to the corral, Ed went into the tack room and came out loaded with gear. He flung a saddle blanket across Shadow's back and heaved the heavy saddle up over it. He gave the sorrel a gentle prod to move aside so that he could fasten the cinch strap and adjust the bridle.

"You'll soon be doing this yourself," he told

Melissa. And he gestured for Melissa to follow as he walked Shadow to the mounting block.

When she stepped up on the block, Ed showed her how to place her left foot in the stirrup. She grasped the saddle horn, and he helped her spring up into the saddle. Then he adjusted the stirrups and handed her the reins.

Mounted on the sorrel, Melissa glanced down at the ground. It seemed miles away. She grabbed the saddle horn and hung onto it tightly as Ed started walking Shadow around the corral.

"How you coming?" he asked, glancing back over his shoulder.

"It f-feels f-funny," Melissa replied in a shaky voice.

The gentle mare that had nibbled sugar from her hand just a moment ago had suddenly changed into a big, unsteady creature with huge, moving muscles that kept shifting her to and fro in the saddle. She clung tighter than ever to the saddle horn as she felt herself swaying precariously back and forth.

Ed shook his head in disapproval. "You learn to guide a horse by the reins, not by the saddle horn. There's a saying that might help you to sit 'light' in your saddle, Missy. It goes like this: 'The head and the heart, keep up. The hands and the heels, keep down. The elbows and the knees, keep in.'"

Melissa took the reins in her hands and tried very hard to follow Ed's advice. She kept her head up, her hands and heels down, her elbows and knees in, and she tried to keep her heart up. Gradually she felt herself relaxing, and Shadow's big, moving muscles became part of the rhythm of the walk. She was beginning to feel "light" in the saddle, just as Ed had said she would.

As they walked the sorrel around the corral, Ed told her all about himself. He lived in a little house trailer next to the horse barn. When he was young, he had been a wrangler on a dude ranch out West. He had come East to live and got this job at the Triple J when Jeff Mathews decided to board and breed horses. There wasn't much he didn't know about horses, he assured her, having been around them all his life.

Ed was an easygoing kind of person, and Melissa liked him. He kept telling her that learning to ride wasn't hard at all and that she was doing just fine. He told her that when she got the feel of her horse, she would begin to think that she was not *on* Shadow but part of her. "That's when riding becomes fun," he said.

After several turns around the corral, he let go the bridle, and Melissa rode by herself. It was just as Ed had told her. She was beginning to feel as though she weren't just *on* Shadow—she was part of the beautiful sorrel.

Her confidence in herself and in her horse must have shown, for when she rode Shadow past the gate where Jan stood watching, she was surprised to glimpse the look of longing on Jan's face. At that moment she knew that Jan was riding with her, feeling the same joy and freedom that she was feeling now as she rode Shadow.

When she came around to Ed again, he showed her how to bring Shadow to an easy halt by closing both legs against the saddle and pulling evenly and gently on the reins. "Never jerk back hard on the lines," he warned. "The bit will cut into Shadow's mouth and will make her rear up. She'll throw you without meaning to."

There were so many things to remember. But it was fun, and Melissa wished that she could keep on riding forever.

Uncle Jeff came to the stable door and nodded with approval as he watched her bring Shadow to an easy halt. "You're doing fine, Missy," he praised. "I'd judge in a day or two you'll be riding around the corral by yourself."

He glanced over at his daughter by the gate as he said this, and Melissa caught the wistful look in his eyes. She also noticed the hurt expression in Jan's eyes.

"Well, it's her own fault that she won't ride," Melissa thought, and turned her attention back to the sorrel.

She reached over in the saddle and gave Shadow a gentle pat. To think that just this morning she had been in New York, saying good-bye to Gran, and now look at her! She was riding her sorrel horse, and she didn't have to imagine it at all. Shadow was as real and beautiful and wonderful as any horse in her dreams.

Best Friends

That night, alone in her room, Melissa thought about home again. She wondered what Mama and Gran were doing now. Were they thinking about her? Did they miss her as much as she was missing them?

Melissa propped herself up in bed and looked out the window into the night. The stars pierced through the sky like bright pinpoints. All else was black. She couldn't see anything—not the horse barn or the pasture or the woods. And it was so quiet. She never knew nights could be so dark and still.

In the city there were neon lights blinking on and off all night and cars and trucks roaring by and people sitting on their stoops in front of the project or standing in the dimly lighted hallways, talking. Once in a while somebody would strum on a guitar, and there would be singing. And sometimes she and Gran would walk down the street to the Sweet Shop and sip iced drinks to keep cool. Nobody seemed to do much sleeping on hot summer nights in her neighborhood.

Melissa kept staring out into the black silence. A light wind rippled the curtains at the window. It touched her face and made her shiver. She pulled the covers up close around her and squeezed her eyes tightly shut. She tried to sleep, but sleep would not come. There was that awful empty feeling in the bottom of her stomach keeping her awake, and it wasn't because she was hungry. A feeling of loneliness gripped her.

"This must be what it feels like to be homesick," she told herself; and knowing that she couldn't lie in bed any longer feeling this way, she got up to search for the light switch.

Maybe if she looked at the pictures of her family that she had brought with her for a time like this, she would feel better. She remembered how much better Gran's calm, smiling face had made her feel on the bus.

"God is always with you and will take care of you," had been Gran's last words to her that morning. Remembering them eased the empty feeling inside her, and she went back to the bed and sat on the edge of it.

"I guess I better learn to put my troubles into God's hands," she told herself and said a silent prayer. "Dear God, help me understand my summer family and this strange new place. I know that you are always with me."

She was still sitting on the bed when Aunt Julie tiptoed into the room.

"Missy, are you still awake?" Aunt Julie asked, sounding surprised.

"Yes, ma'am," Melissa replied in a small voice.

Aunt Julie had left the door open, and a shaft of light from the hall made a bright path across the floor. She sat on the bed next to Melissa and put her hand lightly on Melissa's arm.

"I know how strange the first night in the country must seem to you, Missy." Aunt Julie's voice was gentle with understanding. "But don't think about it. Instead, think about Shadow sleeping in the pasture and about the fun you'll have riding her tomorrow."

"Where does Shadow sleep in the pasture?" Melissa asked, remembering that she had first seen the sorrel by the fence underneath her window.

"Her favorite place is alongside the house." Aunt Julie gave a little laugh. "Do you know why she likes it there?"

Melissa shook her head in the dark, and Aunt Julie went on explaining. "She likes to stand there by the fence so that she can listen to the bamboo wind chimes that hang inside the screen on the side porch. And that's what she's probably doing right now—listening to them in her sleep."

Melissa smiled at the thought of Shadow listening to wind chimes in her sleep.

Aunt Julie stood up. "Come, dear, let me hear your prayers, and then I'll tuck you in."

They stood together in the dark while Melissa said her prayers; then Aunt Julie tucked the covers around her. She bent to give her a kiss, and all at once Melissa felt warm and calm inside, as she did at home when Gran would cuddle up close to her after a bad dream.

"Good night, dear, and sleep well," Aunt Julie said softly as she tiptoed from the room.

Alone in the dark again, Melissa turned her head toward the open window to listen for the wind chimes. For a moment she thought she could hear them tinkling faintly in the night air. She held her breath when next she heard something else. Coming from below her window, it sounded like the soft nickering of a sleepy horse. Could it be the sorrel? she wondered.

She let out her breath. "Shadow!" she whispered. "Oh, Shadow...."

And knowing now that both God and the beautiful sorrel were near, she closed her eyes and fell sound asleep.

Raindrops on the roof awakened her the next morning. In the half-light Melissa threw back the covers and swung her feet to the floor. She shuffled over to the window and looked out. The day was gray and drippy. A low echo of thunder rumbled across the bottom pasture. A drop of rain splashed on her cheek as she leaned over to close the window. Shivering, she hurried to get dressed.

The tantalizing aroma of bacon and eggs greeted her as she made her way down the backstairs. When she stepped into the warm, cheerful kitchen, Jan was already at the breakfast table, waiting for her.

"Hi, sleepyhead. I thought you'd never get up," Jan said as Melissa slipped into her place at the table. "Mom, Dad, and Ed had breakfast ages ago, but Mom wouldn't let me wake you."

"Missy had such a busy day yesterday that I thought a little extra sleep this morning wouldn't matter," Aunt Julie explained with a secretive wink meant just for Melissa. She didn't mention anything about Melissa's being homesick the night before and not being able to sleep.

"Aunt Julie's okay," thought Melissa as she sipped her orange juice. "She knows just the right things to say. Like Gran."

Jan turned her attention to the raindrops streaming down the kitchen windowpane in long zigzag lines. "It would have to rain today!" she said with a sigh.

Through the rain-streaked window the corral, the horse barn, and the pasture were shrouded in gray mist. Everything outside appeared as dismal as Jan looked, and Melissa began to feel gloomy herself at the thought of not being able to ride Shadow.

"Don't look so unhappy, you two," Aunt Julie spoke up brightly. "I have some errands to do in Smithville, and a rainy day is a good time to get them done. Why don't you girls come along?"

Melissa remembered that she wanted to take home something for Mama and Gran from her vacation. Maybe today was her chance to shop for a gift.

"Are there any stores in Smithville?" she asked.

Mrs. Mathews scooped out the eggs from the frying pan and nodded. "There's a department store and a ten-cent store right near the Kandy Kitchen." She flashed Jan a knowing glance. "Sundaes at the Kandy Kitchen are out of this world, aren't they, Janny?"

"Umm, you bet!" Jan's pout quickly vanished. "I guess going to Smithville is better than just sitting around the house all day."

Aunt Julie started to make plans. "Let's have an early lunch so that we can get a good start," she suggested. "I'll make a casserole for dinner tonight and put it in the refrigerator. You girls can start on the jello for dessert. Any flavor you like."

After breakfast they got busy at once. They mixed a box of cherry jello with a box of lemon and cut up pieces of fresh fruit to add to it.

"While we wait for the jello to cool, let's go out and see about the horses," Jan said as she watched Melissa dice the last piece of pineapple.

They ran up the backstairs to wash their sticky hands and straighten up their rooms. Then Melissa followed Jan to the coat closet in the hall, where they found an assortment of raincoats. Choosing two for themselves, they shrugged into them and hurried outside.

Shadow and a spotted mare were standing by the pasture gate, dripping wet, their heads down, waiting to be let into the barn.

"Hi, Patches," Jan called to the spotted mare. The pinto whinnied a greeting and trotted up to the fence where they were standing.

Melissa laughed. "Patches? That's a funny name to give a horse."

"She got that name because her white coat is covered with those large brown spots, and Mom said they look just like brown patches," Jan explained. "She's my favorite horse. Every morning I feed and brush her."

Melissa noticed how fondly Jan stroked the pinto's neck, and she couldn't help asking, "If you like her so much, why don't you ride her?"

She was surprised at Jan's tone of reproof. "Just because I don't ride her doesn't mean that I don't like Patches. I love every one of our horses. I think it's strange that everybody thinks you have to ride horses to like them." And with a pouty look she opened the corral gate and led

Patches and Shadow to the barn.

When they reached the stable with its smells of horses and saddle leather, Jan led Shadow and Patches to their stalls. She ran a rubrag over Patches' wet coat, then brushed the pinto's flanks and combed the tangled mane and tail with a currycomb. Patches dropped her head and began nuzzling the pockets of Jan's jeans as if searching for a cube of sugar or a piece of carrot.

Jan patted the mare's withers and laughed. "You old beggar! You'll soon have your oats."

When Jan started to groom Shadow, Melissa helped. A sedate lady compared to the frisky Patches, Shadow nickered contentedly at all the attention she was getting and stood patiently. As she brushed Shadow's tail and mane with great care, Melissa decided that grooming the beautiful sorrel was the next best thing to riding her.

They weren't alone in the barn. Frieda was making rustling sounds over by the feed bins, and Uncle Jeff and Ed were talking by a silver-gray Arabian mare. Their low voices, dimmed by the rattle of the rain on the barn roof, sounded concerned.

"Princess is about to have a foal any day now," Jan told Melissa. "I guess that's what Dad and Ed are talking about. They usually get pretty anxious when it comes time for a mare to foal."

"I didn't know horses need special attention when their foals are born," Melissa said.

"Princess is different," Jan explained. "She's a

thoroughbred and very high strung. If anything ever happened to her or her foal, Dad and Ed would feel terrible. And, wow, so would I!"

Melissa glanced over at Princess and saw Uncle Jeff lay a gentle hand on the mare's full side. Then he closed the gate to her stall and went about his work. Ed filled the feedbox and started to muck out the stall.

The girls turned back to their own work. Melissa was standing on tiptoe, reaching up to smooth Shadow's wet forelock, when she felt something butting hard against her back. Surprised, she let the currycomb fly out of her hand and swung around to see what had struck her. There was Patches, craning her head over the side of the stall and whinnying through her big yellow teeth.

Jan looked up with a frown and gave the pinto a slap across the muzzle. "Butting is her one bad habit, and Dad says I have to break her of it."

Patches tossed her head saucily, shook her mane, and blew through her muzzle at Jan. She looked so indignant that both girls couldn't help but laugh.

After they had finished grooming the horses and had made sure the feedboxes and water buckets were filled, Jan gave Melissa a tour of the stable. "There's Black Lightning," she said, pointing to a beautiful black stallion, who raised his head from his feedbox and watched them with intelligent brown eyes. "He's one of the finest thoroughbreds in the state. Dad boards him for a man in the city who comes weekends to ride him."

"Does your father board Shadow and Patches too?" Melissa asked as they walked past the other stalls.

"No, they're our own horses. So is Princess." Jan's eyes brightened. "Dad said that when her foal is born, I can have it to raise as my own colt. I'll just love taking care of it. Oh, Missy, colts are so cute. I hope it's born while you're here."

As they entered the tack room at the far end of the stable, Melissa thought about Jan and her new colt. Wouldn't exercising and training it be part of raising it? she wondered. And wouldn't Jan have to ride the colt for that?

The tack room was filled with saddles and saddle blankets, bridles, ropes, and halters. The shelves contained saddle soap, sponges, cans of horse liniment, and first-aid equipment. The girls put their brushes and currycombs on a bottom shelf, then hurried back to the house through the rain. Aunt Julie was putting the fruit into their jello when they flung themselves into the kitchen like two wet puppies.

"Run upstairs, both of you, and get ready," she said. "We'll leave for Smithville right after lunch."

Melissa changed into her new pink shorts and white blouse. She opened her purse to make sure she still had the five dollars Mama had given her for spending money. She had planned to use some of the money to buy Mama and Gran's present.

When they left the house a half hour later, Frieda was waiting for them outside the kitchen door. She wagged her tail and whined hopefully as Aunt Julie backed the station wagon out of the garage.

"Every time somebody drives off, Frieda begs to go along," Jan told Melissa as they slid into the front seat next to Aunt Julie, "but we can't take her today because we'll be gone too long."

Frieda barked frantically and raced alongside the car as it started up the lane. When she got tired of chasing, she sat in the middle of the road and cocked her head dolefully as she watched them go off without her. She looked so forlorn at being left behind that Melissa turned to wave to her.

On the way to Smithville they talked about all the things they planned to do there. Aunt Julie said she had groceries to buy and a few things at the department store. The girls decided that the ten-cent store would be a good place to shop for Melissa's present. They would save their treat at the Kandy Kitchen until last.

The station wagon slowed down for a turn in the road, and through the rain-splashed windshield Melissa glimpsed the tall white spire of a church up ahead.

"We're coming to Smithville," Jan announced.

The little village looked just like the quaint towns the bus had passed through yesterday. As they drove by each pretty frame or brick house, surrounded by flower gardens and pleasant green lawns, Melissa wondered whether it might be the house where Rosita was staying. She wondered what Rosita was doing this rainy day. Probably sitting in front of the color TV, eating popsicles.

The thought made Melissa smile, but she was glad Pastor Dan had decided that the Triple J would be the place for her this summer. What were popsicles and color TV compared to Shadow!

They had come to the center of the town and were passing a scattering of shops, a post office, and a bank. Aunt Julie found a parking place in the lot behind the department store.

"Meet me here in about an hour," she called to Jan, who had already slipped out of the station wagon and was limping hurriedly through the rain to the ten-cent store down the street. Melissa observed that when Jan was excited or in a hurry, her limp was more noticeable.

"Hurry, Missy," Jan flung back over her shoulder, "or we'll get soaked."

The wonderful smells of perfume and popcorn and the spicy aroma of hot dogs sizzling on a grill greeted them as they entered the store. A record was playing the latest rock 'n' roll. Cash registers jingled merrily. Long counters of attractive merchandise stretched out before them.

They stopped to look at the long strands of colored beads at the end of the jewelry counter. They walked past the gay ribbons and scarves. They wandered on, entranced, from one counter to another until they found themselves in the pet department at the rear of the store.

"Why not buy your mom and grandmother a tropical fish?" Jan suggested, pointing to the tiny colorful fish swimming around in the aquarium. "You could put it in one of those little glass bowls and buy a china castle for the fish's home."

Melissa looked longingly at a beautiful black and gold fish with its wavering, fan-like tail. It darted in and out among the water plants at the bottom of the tank, then swam to the top and opened its mouth in a round O for air. She'd just love to have a fish like that, but would Mama and Gran want one? After all, this was to be their present, not hers.

"How could I take a fish home with me on the bus?" she rationalized. "The water would spill all over the place."

"I hadn't thought of that," Jan said. "They sure are pretty, though."

Next to the fish tank was a cage of canaries. The girls stepped in front of the cage to watch the birds. The canaries fluttered their yellow wings and sang in gay, fluted voices.

"Once they had some parakeets here," Jan told Melissa. "And one of them could talk. He'd keep saying, 'Hello, pretty boy! Hello, pretty boy!'"

Jan made a face. "Who'd call a boy *pretty!*"

"Yeah, I know!" Melissa replied, giggling.

They wandered back toward the front of the store. Melissa gave a long sigh. She'd had no idea that it would be so hard to decide on a gift for Mama and Gran. There were so many things to look at, yet so far she hadn't seen anything she wanted to buy for them.

Her eyes wandered over a counter of glass vases and china bric-a-brac. It was then that she spied the little china horse half hidden between a large glass vase and a fancy teapot. She stared at the figurine for a long minute before reaching out and carefully picking it up.

"Oh, look!" she breathed, holding the little horse out for Jan to see. Its shining coat was a light chestnut color. It had a golden tail and flowing mane, and its tiny black hooves were spread apart as though it were trotting.

"Why, it looks just like Shadow!" Jan exclaimed, staring at the figurine.

"I know," Melissa murmured. Even the white blaze running down its tiny muzzle was Shadow's.

"Do you think your mom and grandmother would like it?"

Melissa hesitated. Would they like it or had she just *thought* they would because she herself liked it?

But Melissa couldn't put the china horse back

on the counter. She just had to hold it close to her. It seemed to belong in her hands.

"I'll tell them this is how Shadow looks," she explained to Jan. "Then I'm sure they'll like it."

"Okay, buy it," Jan urged. She had been hoping Melissa would choose the china horse, and after the cashier had wrapped it, she said, "Now, let's get the sundaes. I'm starved!"

Aunt Julie was waiting in the station wagon when they arrived at the parking lot at the end of their hour. "Hop in," she called. "It's getting late." The motor whirred to a start.

"Did you find a present for your mother and grandmother, Missy?" she asked as she backed the car out of the lot.

Melissa drew the china horse from its wrappings to show her.

"Why, it's lovely," Aunt Julie said.

Melissa ran a finger over the china horse. If Aunt Julie liked it, she felt certain that Mama and Gran would also like it.

"I bought some presents too," remarked Aunt Julie. "They are in the back in pink bags, one for each of you."

The girls turned quickly and spied the two small bags lying in the corner of the backseat. "Oh wow, Mom, can we open them now?" asked Jan.

Aunt Julie maneuvered a turn in the road and nodded.

They reached back for the bags and with eager

fingers opened them. A small square box was inside each bag. Jan opened her box first. For a second she just stared at what was inside. Then she cried, "Oh—look!" and held up a charm bracelet with a silver heart dangling from it. "It's a friendship bracelet. I've always wanted one!"

Melissa quickly opened her box. She was hoping her present would be a friendship bracelet like Jan's. And it was!

Gently Melissa fingered the little charm. Never before had she received such a lovely gift. She examined the silver heart closely and noticed that a tiny M was engraved in the middle of it.

"Look, my initial is on my charm," she told Jan. Then they both examined Jan's charm and found a tiny J on hers.

"Oh, Missy," Jan cried delightedly, "we both have friendship bracelets alike. That means we're best friends."

"I know," Melissa breathed. They looked at one another and smiles filled their faces.

Melissa glanced down again at the friendship bracelet, then out through the rain-streaked car window. Never had a rainy day turned out to be so wonderful, she decided. And it wasn't only because of the china horse she had found for Mama and Gran, and Aunt Julie's lovely gift. It was because of what Jan had just said.

With a rush of happiness Melissa knew that she had found another best friend.

No Longer a Dude

Melissa wore her friendship bracelet to bed that night. She wanted to feel it on her wrist, close to her, while she slept. And when she opened her eyes the next morning, it was the first thing she saw. She jiggled her arm, making the little silver heart sparkle against her wrist. At breakfast Jan confessed that she had not taken off her bracelet either last night.

After helping Aunt Julie clear the table and do the dishes, they went to the barn to look for Ed. They found him in the tack room, polishing saddles. Frieda was curled up on the floor by his feet. When she saw the girls, she lifted her big head and thumped her tail expectantly.

Jan held out her wrist. "Look what we got, Ed. They're friendship bracelets, which means that Missy and I are best friends."

Ed examined the initials on each charm. "Well, now, that's real nice. A best friend's a thing to treasure, that's for sure. They don't come that plentiful."

He looked knowingly at Melissa and his smile widened. "I reckon you didn't come here just to show off that bracelet, Missy. Help me put an extra shine on these saddles," he went on, nodding toward the row of saddles lined up on the saddle rack. "Then I'll teach you a few more riding tricks."

His eyes turned toward Jan. "I'll ride Patches. She doesn't get much exercise."

Melissa's eyes sought Jan, too, in a long, hesitating look. Now that they were best friends, she didn't want to do anything to hurt Jan. "Maybe we could go swimming first," she said.

"Oh, that's okay," Jan replied, still looking at her bracelet. "I know how much you like to ride Shadow, Missy. Anyway, I promised Dad I'd muck out Little Darling's stall today. He's taking the palomino to the Miller farm this morning."

Before she left the tack room, she called back, "We'll go swimming after you finish your ride, Missy." She grabbed a brush and pail and went to the palomino's empty stall.

Ed shook his head as he watched her go. "I sure wish Jan would get over that fear of riding. I know that Jeff wants more than anything in the world to see his daughter ride. And she loves that little pinto of hers," he added, handing Melissa a cake of saddle soap and a sponge. "She'd be a good rider if she'd only try." He paused and his blue-gray eyes studied Melissa thoughtfully. "I've been hoping that when she sees you riding Shadow and enjoying it so much, she'll want to ride bad enough to forget her fear. Do you think you can help her, Missy?"

Melissa frowned down at the saddle she was polishing. "Is that why you want to teach me to ride Shadow?"

"Partly," Ed replied frankly. "But the main reason is that I know you got horse fever, girl, and I had it just as bad myself when I was your age."

She smiled up at Ed, knowing that he was being honest with her.

Ed grinned back and put his rag and can of neat's-foot oil on the shelf. "That's all for today," he told her. "Now let's get Shadow and I'll show you how to tack up."

Ed took a saddle from the rack, and Melissa carried the bridle and saddle blanket to the corral where Shadow was waiting for them. Ed showed her how to slip the bit between Shadow's teeth and bring the bridle up over the sorrel's head and ears. Standing on the mounting block, she had no trouble flinging the saddle blanket across Shadow's back, but it took an effort to lift the heavy saddle onto the blanket. Ed instructed her how to bring the cinch strap around Shadow's belly to hold the saddle on and how to tighten the cinch just right.

When Shadow was bridled and saddled, Ed walked around the horse to examine the tack. "You're no longer a dude, Missy," he said with satisfaction.

"What's a dude, Ed?"

"Oh, that's a person who is new around horses and hasn't saddled up yet. When a rider can bridle and saddle her own horse, she's no longer a dude. Now hop back on that mounting block, and let's see what you remember from the other day."

Melissa stepped up on the block. Placing her left foot in the stirrup, she grasped the saddle horn with both hands and stretched herself up into the saddle. Trying to remember what Ed had taught her, she sat down and forward in her saddle, head up, hands and heels down, elbows and knees in. Ed gave her a wink of approval as he mounted Patches, and side by side they walked their mounts around the corral until Melissa got the feel of her saddle.

"Never let the reins go slack or give Shadow her head," he told her. "She'll go racing around the corral at any gait she takes a fancy to if you do. Remember, you're the boss!"

Melissa held the reins more firmly in her hands, but she had her doubts as to who was really the boss, she or the sorrel.

Ed showed her how to turn and back her mount, and after she had practiced several times, he told her to press both legs behind the cinch strap and to ease up on the reins a little. When Melissa did this, Shadow emerged from her easy walk to a lively jog. Melissa found herself bumping up and down on the sorrel like a jumping jack. It felt just like being spanked every time she hit the hard saddle.

Ed laughed as he watched her go. Melissa supposed it did look funny, her bouncing up and down in the saddle this way. But it didn't feel very funny!

Ed called to her to rise in the saddle to the rhythm of Shadow's trot. "Up, down—up, down—easy does it," his voice sang out. Following Ed's advice, she discovered that she was bouncing less awkwardly.

"Now you're learning how to post," Ed told her. He grinned his approval as he watched her begin to jog smoothly around the corral.

It was fun following the motion of the trotting horse, with the wind brushing softly against her face and the muffled sound of hoofbeats on the soft turf. As she rose in the saddle to the easy rhythm of Shadow's jogging, Melissa felt, more than ever, that she wasn't just mounted on Shadow—she was part of the graceful sorrel.

Out of the corner of her eye she noticed Jan watching her from the doorway of the tack room. Again Melissa glimpsed the wistful look on Jan's face, and a sudden thought struck her: "Jan *really* does want to ride." As Ed had said, it was fear alone that kept Jan from the saddle.

Melissa turned her attention to her jogging mount. She was now thoroughly enjoying Shadow's brisk trot and hoped that when Jan saw how much fun she was having, she would forget her fear and want to ride too.

At last Ed called her to halt and watched with satisfaction as she reined in Shadow, bringing the sorrel to a clean, easy stop. "How would you like to ride to the high pasture with me to check the fences?" he asked her. "It's an easy enough ride for a beginner."

Catching the bright excitement in her eyes, he swung off his mount and opened the corral gate. Mounting Patches again, he led the way out of the corral, and they walked their horses across the meadow behind the barn.

Shadow followed in a slow, easy gait. The sun shone golden on her coat; the breeze ruffled her mane; the tall grass made soft swishing sounds against her long, slender legs. Her head bobbed up and down to the rhythm of her gait.

They rode up a gently sloping hill where several horses grazed, their graceful shapes silhouetted against the green of the high pasture. At the top they reined in their mounts and looked out over the farm.

Melissa felt as if she were on top of the world. The wide sweep of sky curved over her like an enormous blue canopy. In a field on the other side of the fence, the herd of cattle grazed, and at the bottom was the cattle barn. Beyond, the countryside spread out in gentle ripples of valleys and tall hills. A long level range of blue mountains shimmered in the distance. The landscape was so vast, so still that Melissa thought she could even hear her heart beat. It was Ed's voice that broke the silence around them.

"See that wide break in that blue mountain over yonder?" he said, pointing. "Well, that's the Delaware Water Gap. The Delaware River, that separates New Jersey from Pennsylvania, flows beneath it."

"I didn't know Pennsylvania was so close," Melissa said.

Ed pointed next to a wooded slope across the road from the house. "That woods has one of the best riding trails in New Jersey," he boasted. "The Smithville Saddle Club will be riding all ten miles of it the end of this week. Then they'll come here to the Triple J for the gymkhana."

Melissa looked baffled. "The gym—what?"

Ed laughed. "Oh, I forgot. Being a city girl, you probably don't know what a gymkhana is. Well, it's a fun day the Saddle Club has once a year when they play games with their horses. This year you'll be here for it."

Melissa was more bewildered than ever. "How do you play games with horses?" she asked. She couldn't imagine playing kickball or a game of

Frisbee with Shadow. The thought struck her funny and she burst into laughter.

"Oh, the games are mostly races," Ed hastened to explain. "There's the flag race, the barrel race, the ribbon race, the break-your-gait-or-out race—all kinds of events. And there are prizes for each race."

"What weird-sounding names for races," Melissa said, "but the gym-whatever-it-is sounds neat."

"It sure is," replied Ed, chuckling. "The funniest race is the egg race."

"Oh, wow! Now I've heard everything!" Melissa laughed again. "An egg race—with horses?"

"It's the race for fourteen-year-old kids and younger," Ed explained. "Jeff calls out the different gaits you have to put your horse through, like walking, jogging, or riding in reverse and backing up. And while you're putting your horse through those gaits, you have to carry an egg on a spoon. The last rider with the egg still on his spoon wins."

Melissa shook her head unbelievingly. "Carrying an egg on a spoon while riding! You got to be kidding! I know any egg I held would be scrambled before I even got started!"

Melissa felt as if she were on top of the world. The landscape was so vast, so still that Melissa thought she could even hear her heart beat.

"I know, it's hard," Ed admitted, laughing, "but it's a lot of fun trying, even though hardly anyone gets through the jog with the egg still on his spoon."

They turned their horses' heads and walked them side by side around the high pasture while Ed inspected the fence. "I wish Princess could be in the gymkhana this year," he went on. "She and Jeff usually win a prize in the jumping contest. Princess is our thoroughbred Arabian and the best jumper in the club. But she's going to have a foal any day now, so that's why Jeff can't ride her."

"I know," Melissa replied. "Jan said that her father's going to give her the colt."

"Yup," Ed nodded. "Jeff hopes that Jan will learn to love that little colt so much that she'll want to ride it when it gets big enough."

"I guess it means a lot to him to have Jan ride again," Melissa murmured.

"It's more than just having Jan ride again, Missy," Ed explained. "You see, Jeff took it real hard when that fall from the horse left Jan crippled and frightened. He sort of blames himself for having her ride so early. Jan's limp is getting better the older she gets, but her fear of riding is just as great as ever. And it's keeping her from a lot of fun that the kids her age around here are having. She's growing more and more into her shell the older she gets because of it."

Melissa nodded soberly. She knew what Ed

74

meant. She herself knew how important it was to be able to join in with the other kids in school or youth center activities. It would be awful to feel left out of things.

They rode the rest of the way around the high pasture. Then Ed said, "We best be getting back. Tomorrow we'll do a little trail-riding if you like, Missy."

"You mean," Melissa blurted out happily, "I'm good enough for that?"

"Sure you are," Ed told her. "You're no longer a tenderfoot."

Melissa felt a pride she had never felt before as they walked their horses down to the corral gate. Trail-riding with Shadow! Not only was she no longer a dude, but she was no longer a tenderfoot. And Ed knew it.

Audrey

Don't tell me it's going to rain again!" Jan scowled up at the threatening sky. For the last half hour while they had been swimming, they had tried to ignore the ominous black clouds that were gathering over the treetops. But when lightning flashed and thunder groaned and a wet wind started blowing across the kill pool, they couldn't ignore the coming storm any longer. They gathered up their towels and fled through the woods and across the pasture. They made it to the house just as the first big drops came pelting down on their backs.

Aunt Julie was standing by the stove, making blueberry pancakes. She flipped over the first four pancakes, then set them on the table. "It's only a shower, I believe," she said as if she were trying to justify the faulty weather conditions. "It's been so warm and humid after yesterday's rain that we need a good shower to clear the atmosphere."

Uncle Jeff smiled as the girls took their places at the table. "One good thing—every time it rains, Mother makes blueberry pancakes for lunch," he told them. "Help yourself, Missy. Hmm, are they delicious!"

Dripping with butter and syrup, the pancakes *were* delicious, and after her ride with Ed and her swim in the kill, Melissa had an enormous appetite for lunch that day. As she started on her third pancake, she told everybody, "If I keep this up, Dr. Emory won't be calling me a skinny old bean pole much longer." Aunt Julie laughed and slipped another pancake onto her plate.

After lunch the girls helped with the dishes, then went upstairs to Jan's room.

"I have a new album," Jan said, leafing through the stack of records by her stereo. "Would you like to hear it?"

Melissa shrugged. "Okay." And she walked over to look at the doll collection on the window seat while Jan fiddled with the stereo.

She picked up a pretty doll dressed in a white, peaked cap and wooden shoes. "Where did this one come from?" she asked.

"That's Gretchen, my Dutch doll from

Holland, Michigan," Jan told her. She put a record on the turntable and snapped her fingers to the music.

Melissa examined the funny little wooden shoes and the white, peaked cap that the Dutch doll wore. While the record played, Jan showed her the other dolls. There was an Indian doll dressed in soft doeskin, with a white feather in a beaded headband around her shiny dark hair.

"Her name is White Feather," Jan said. "And this is Lem, my favorite. He's a cowboy doll that Ed brought me from Texas."

They took the dolls and sat on the bed. Jan picked up Lem and spoke for him in a Western drawl, "How you-all like that record, Missy?"

"Yeah, man, it's real cool," replied Melissa laughing.

"What kind of talk is that?" drawled Lem in Jan's voice.

"That's East Side talk, baby," Melissa answered. "That's where I come from. Man, I don't dig you. Where you from?"

"I'm from Texas," replied Lem. "And I don't dig you much either."

The girls broke into wild giggles. Above the sounds of the stereo and their laughter, they didn't hear a car drive up the lane and stop in front of the house. Not until the kitchen door slammed shut and they heard the sound of hurried footsteps on the stairs did they stop their giggling and turn down the stereo. The next moment a girl in a bright blue rain cape burst into the room.

"Audrey!" cried Jan with happy surprise. "I didn't know you were coming."

"I didn't either until a half hour ago," the girl replied breathlessly. She took off her cape, tossed it over a chair, and flung back her long auburn hair so that it fell over her shoulders like a shimmering red shawl. "It was so rainy that Daddy couldn't work outside, so he decided to come talk about the gymkhana with your father. I came along because I have something to tell you."

She paused and stared at Melissa and the dolls scattered over the bed. "Don't tell me you're playing with *dolls!*"

"Of course not—" Jan started to explain but changed her mind and said instead, "Audrey, this is Missy Howard, my Fresh Air friend from New York City. Missy, Audrey is my friend I've been telling you about."

Melissa could feel the girl's bright hazel eyes wandering curiously over her. When they rested on the charm bracelet she was wearing, they were cold and disapproving.

"You both have friendship bracelets alike!" Audrey cried with surprise. "Do you know what that means, Jan?"

Jan threw her friend a quick look and nodded. Melissa ran her hand protectively over the heart-shaped charm. There was something about this girl that made her feel uneasy.

Audrey's eyes narrowed as she glanced from one charm bracelet to the other. She swung around and stared at Jan accusingly, her voice rising to a high shrill. "You must be kidding!"

Jan's face turned red. She hesitated, looking confused. Then she explained hastily, "Mom bought them for us yesterday in Smithville—as a surprise."

"Oh." Audrey tossed her head and let the subject drop. Raising her eyebrows at Jan in a mocking gesture, she said airily, "I don't suppose you'll be riding in the gymkhana this week."

Jan sat frozen and didn't reply.

A tight feeling rose in Melissa's throat. If Audrey was Jan's best friend in Smithville, why was she talking to her like that? And what did Audrey mean when she said Jan must be kidding about the friendship bracelets? Was she implying that it would be impossible for Jan to be best friends with a girl who lived in a city housing project?

Melissa drew her arms tight around her knees. "Well, she doesn't have to like me for all I care," she told herself as she returned Audrey's disapproving stare. "And I don't have to like people who don't like me, either."

Immediately a Bible verse she had once memorized flashed through her mind: "Do unto others as you would have them do unto you." And suddenly she realized that she was thinking this way because she herself was afraid of not being liked.

Audrey flopped down on the bed next to Jan and babbled on as if nothing had happened. "What I wanted to tell you is that Daddy bought me a palomino gelding at the horse auction last week. Oh, Jan, he has the most beautiful gold-colored coat, and Daddy said I could ride him in the gymkhana on Saturday. You can see him then."

"What's his name?" Jan asked in a voice full of relief now that Audrey had turned the subject around to herself and her new horse.

"He's called Silver Beauty, and he has the most beautiful silvery white mane and tail. He has a white blaze and white stockings too. Oh, he's so—scrumptious!" Audrey closed her eyes and looked blissful as she described her horse.

She chattered on as if Melissa didn't exist. "She's one of 'those others' that Gran talks about," Melissa told herself. She remembered girls like Audrey in school last year. They were always pushing everybody around and thinking they knew it all and were better than anyone else. She wondered how girls like that got to be so popular.

Melissa fidgeted and twisted her finger around the Indian doll's tiny white feather. She wished she could slip away to her own room and not have to listen to Audrey's silly chatter. She and Jan had been having so much fun until Audrey appeared on the scene!

When Audrey finally ran out of conversation,

Jan played more records until Aunt Julie called up the stairs that Mr. Van Doren was leaving.

Audrey jumped up and whisked her rain cape off the chair. "See you both at the gymkhana!" were her haunting last words as she sailed out of the room.

Jan didn't follow her friend downstairs. Instead, she stood quietly by the window and watched with a frown as Audrey got into her father's big station wagon and drove off.

Then, without a word to Melissa, she turned and left the room.

"I Don't Belong Here!"

At dinner that evening Jan hardly spoke a word. She was polite enough, passing the food and even smiling, but there was something stiff and unnatural about her smile. It was as if she were holding herself back from Melissa, as if an invisible barrier had suddenly sprung up between them. And when Jan passed the rolls, Melissa noticed for the first time that she wasn't wearing her friendship bracelet.

As soon as dinner was over, Melissa slipped outside. She crossed the yard to the pasture fence to look for the sorrel. Now, more than anything else, she wanted to be alone with Shadow.

The rain-washed pasture smelled fresh and

sweet after the storm. Pink clouds, like cotton candy, were spun across the sky. The low afternoon sun etched rosy-colored tree patterns on the side of the house. Into the patterns stepped the shadow of a horse.

Melissa remembered what Aunt Julie had told her about Shadow's liking to stand by the fence to listen to the bamboo wind chimes that hung inside the screen on the side porch. And that's what the sorrel was doing now—listening to the chimes tinkling faintly in the soft breeze. When she heard Melissa coming, she lifted her head and neighed a welcome.

Melissa slipped through the rails of the fence and held out a sugar cube. The soft, velvety muzzle against her hand made her feel warm inside. She put her head against Shadow's shoulder, and for a long time they stood together, Melissa scarcely noticing the dipping sun and the darkness that was beginning to creep up from the woods and across the pasture.

It was so quiet, so peaceful, that the sudden sound of voices rising on the evening air gave Melissa a start. She pressed closer to Shadow's side, so close that she could feel the sorrel's steady heartbeat.

The voices drifted from the screened-in porch out across the yard. They mingled with the clinking of the wind chimes, but Melissa couldn't help hearing what they said. It was like listening to an unseen drama, as if somebody had turned up the volume on a television set and she could hear the voices but could not see the faces.

She recognized Uncle Jeff's voice first. "Can't you remember how happy and excited you were that Missy was coming? Why this sudden change of heart?" he was asking.

There was a click of high heels across the porch; then Aunt Julie spoke. "It's because of Audrey, isn't it, dear? It's something Audrey said this afternoon."

Silence. Then Aunt Julie said, "Don't you know, honey, that there are more important things in this world than what others think or say?"

"I know, Mom." Jan's voice sounded confused and unhappy. "But it does matter what Audrey thinks. Audrey is the most popular girl in school, and—and she's my best friend."

"You never let the gymkhana bother you other years," Uncle Jeff joined in.

"Well, Audrey never said anything about my not riding then," Jan replied. "It's—it's different this year. All the kids will be here and they all ride and—and all of a sudden it means so much to everybody."

Silence again. Then the click of heels moving back across the porch and Aunt Julie saying impatiently, "Oh, Audrey probably feels that everybody has to be just like her and do exactly as she does. Some very popular girls are like that, you know. But you have to do your own thing, Jan. A real friend likes you for yourself and not just because you do what she wants you to do."

Aunt Julie paused. When she resumed, there was an uplift to her voice. "Anyway, honey, you won't be alone at the gymkhana this year. Missy will be with you."

Jan's high, thin voice pierced the air like shattered glass. "Oh, Missy! Who's she, Mom? Just some poor kid from the city. What does she know about my friends?"

Melissa was stunned. "I don't believe it," she whispered to herself. "I just don't believe I'm hearing all this!" Yesterday Jan had said they were best friends. Now Jan was telling her mother that she was just some poor kid who didn't know anything.

Melissa didn't want to hear any more. She wanted to shut out their voices. She wished she could turn them off as you would turn off the TV.

But Uncle Jeff's voice, edged with anger, seemed to rise out through the screen at her. "Just because Missy's disadvantaged and from the city shouldn't make her any less a friend than your friends here, Jan. And she's every bit as good as Audrey. Besides, she's our guest and it's up to us, especially you, to make her stay with us a pleasant one—regardless of what Audrey thinks."

"Oh, all right," Jan muttered. "After all, she'll only be here two weeks."

Melissa cupped her hand tightly over her

charm bracelet. How could she think of Jan as one of her best friends now after what she had just heard! She unfastened the bracelet and let it slip into the pocket of her jeans.

Rigid, unhappy, afraid to run off for fear of letting them know she was there and had heard, Melissa squeezed her eyes tightly shut and wished the voices would go away. And at last, with relief, she heard their murmuring drift back into the house. She listened to the last faint echo of a syllable fade away into the night; then she flung her arms around Shadow's neck and pressed her face against the warm, soft shoulder.

"I don't belong here," she whispered into the pointed ears that pricked back and forth. "I belong back in the city—back in the project with Mama and Gran and Harriet and Carmen. Oh, Shadow, I wish we could both go there together—now!"

There it didn't matter if your best friends were "disadvantaged," as Uncle Jeff put it. There nobody had to make excuses for you or feel that being your friend would hurt him.

Why had Mama and Gran sent her away this summer? Didn't they know this would happen?

Shadow dropped her head to graze. She lifted one forefoot and then the other. In the growing darkness Melissa could barely make out the sorrel's shadowy form moving off into the pasture.

She was beginning to feel very much alone; then Gran's parting words echoed in her mind as if a voice were speaking them. "God is always with you."

"Oh, God," she murmured, "what has gone wrong with Jan? Can you help me understand it, God?"

The Haunted Mill

Usually when things went wrong at home—when she had a fight with Harriet or Carmen—Melissa would think about tomorrow, a new day, when everything would be right again. But the next morning when she awoke, Melissa wondered if anything would ever be right again between her and Jan.

She stiffly pulled on her clothes and went downstairs. She was late for breakfast this morning, and the kitchen was empty. Aunt Julie was probably in the henhouse feeding her chickens—it was a chore she did first thing every morning—and Jan was probably in the barn grooming Patches. A bowl of cereal, a glass of juice, and a doughnut had been left for her, and she sat down to breakfast alone.

After rinsing off her dishes, she hurried outside hoping that she would not have to talk with anyone. She crossed the side yard and felt a stab of disappointment that Shadow wasn't at her usual place by the fence. Without the sorrel here to greet her, the morning seemed extra empty.

Maybe she'd find Shadow by the kill, she thought. She slipped through the bars of the fence and found herself hurrying across the pasture. The busy tinkling of a metal dog tag betrayed the fact that Frieda was following. Melissa turned to wait for the dog.

Like a black cloud moving across the sunlit field, the big German shepherd came lolloping after her. Melissa reached out to lay a hand on the shaggy head. She was glad for the company. The plume of tail wagged furiously, and together they walked toward the gate to the forest trail.

The woods were fragrant with the spicy odor of pines in the hot sun. A breeze murmured through the thick boughs in a hushed *ahhh*, and from up ahead, where the dim greenery of the trees opened into the sunny glade, came the music of the waterfall. She settled herself on a sun-warmed rock along the grassy bank of the kill to wait for Shadow.

Frieda stretched out by her side, panting, her red tongue lolling affably in that silly big grin of hers. But she did not remain at Melissa's side for long. Her pointed ears pricked forward at a rustling sound in the bushes nearby, and with a sharp bark she was off through the trees on an expedition of her own.

Melissa bent over the rock to observe a dragonfly that had lighted near her hand. It remained perfectly still, shimmering green and blue and golden in the sunlight. Its long iridescent wings fluttered slightly in the moving air, and its thin blue tail jutted out from the end of the beetle-shaped body like a long darning needle. The sudden splash of a fish leaping out of the kill sent the dragonfly whirling over the pool like a miniature helicopter.

Melissa turned her gaze to the widening ripples of water. She gazed down through silvery shafts of sunlight into the depths of the pool, where long filmy water plants swayed to and fro. A school of minnows swam in waves of graceful motion over green mossy stones. The minnows were so tiny, even smaller than the tropical fish in the ten-cent store.

A loud croak nearby made her jump, and a second later she glimpsed a green frog with bulging eyes leap into the water. The minnows darted back and forth, scattering in every direction as the frog burrowed into the muddy bank and sent up a dull brown cloud through the sunlit water.

Melissa looked up again trying to find the dragonfly, and her attention was caught by a strange-looking insect, with long threadlike legs, darting jerkily back and forth on the smooth surface of the pool. How could it stay on top of the water like that? she marveled.

She was still trying to figure it out when she heard the bushes parting behind her. She whirled around, hoping to see Shadow standing there, but it was Jan. The girl limped to the bank and stood awkwardly by the rock, her arms drooping at her sides.

"Hi," she said. "Mom thought I'd find you here. What are you doing?"

Melissa didn't say anything but glanced back across the pool. Jan didn't have to be nice to her just because her parents wanted her to, she thought touchily. She kept staring at the long-legged insect, skittering back and forth over the surface of the water, without really seeing it. She could feel Jan's gaze following hers.

"That's a water strider," Jan said at last. "Do you know how it stays up on top of the pool like that? It's because its legs are so long, thin, and light—like pieces of thread—and they hold it up."

She kicked off her shoes and rolled up her jeans. "It's near shore. I'm going to see if I can catch it. Oh-h-h, this feels good!" she squealed as she stepped into the cold water. "Come on, help me catch it. I won't hurt it. I just want to show it to you up close."

Melissa kept staring blankly ahead until Jan splashed right in front of her and she had to watch.

"Come on," Jan urged again.

"Do unto others. . . ." Did Jan know that Bible verse too?

On sudden impulse Melissa kicked off her sneakers and stepped gingerly into the icy water. Slipping about over the mossy stones at the bottom, they tried to catch the water strider. When at last they came close to it, Jan reached out a cupped hand and lunged forward. Losing her balance on the slippery stones, she went splashing into the pool. The water strider skittered away on its long threadlike legs to the safety of deep water.

"Oh-h-h!" gasped Jan, dripping as she stood up. She looked so funny that Melissa couldn't help but giggle.

Jan looked up at the same time and their eyes met. Without becoming aware of what was happening, they found themselves both laughing. It was as if Jan's dunking had washed away all the tension between them, and now more than anything else they wanted to have fun together. At that moment nothing else seemed to matter.

Jan splashed out of the pool and shook the water from her long hair like a dog. "Come back to the house with me, Missy, while I get into something dry," she said. "Then let's bike out to the old mill. Mom said she'd pack us a lunch for a picnic in the woods."

On the way across the pasture Melissa asked, "What's the old mill?"

"It used to be a gristmill, and it's back in the woods across the road," Jan explained. "It's a huge, gray stone building with a wooden waterwheel alongside it. It's sort of falling apart and covered with vines. Nobody uses it anymore, and hardly anybody goes out that way. It's supposed to be haunted."

"Haunted?" asked Melissa in a quickly drawn breath.

Jan nodded and squinted across the meadow as she tried to recall the details of the mystery. "The old story goes that a long time ago two men who lived in Smithville fell in love with the same girl, and she couldn't decide which one she wanted to marry. The suitors were terribly jealous of one another, and neither would give up the girl, so they decided to settle it all by dueling at the old mill."

Melissa rolled her eyes. "Sounds romantic."

"Well, maybe," Jan said, "but I guess it was pretty awful when they arrived at the mill yard with guns early one morning and paced off so many steps, then turned and fired at one another."

"You mean shooting it out like they do in the Westerns on TV?" Melissa asked curiously. "I didn't know they did those things around here."

"They don't anymore," Jan replied. "That was two hundred years ago. Anyway, to get back to the mystery, Henry Dunbar, the suitor who lost the duel, crawled inside the old mill and died there. At least, that's where they found his body. After the mill became deserted, the old-timers who used to live around there claimed they could hear strange moaning and wailing sounds inside the mill. They said it was Henry Dunbar's ghost, and that it would always haunt the mill as long as it was left standing.

"What was so weird," Jan continued, "was that the girl they were fighting over had become so worked up over the duel that she never married anybody."

"Why don't the people in Smithville tear down the old mill?" Melissa reasoned, "Then maybe the ghost will disappear."

Jan shook her head. "They just don't want to be bothered, I guess. Besides, most folks these days don't believe in ghosts. Mom has even said that somebody ought to restore the old mill as a historical landmark. She and Dad and Ed just laugh when they hear stories that it's haunted."

"Do you think it is?" Melissa asked in a breathless voice.

Jan shrugged. "I don't really believe in ghosts. But—I don't know."

"What do you mean, you don't know?" prodded Melissa.

"Well, this spring some kids from school hiked out there and said they heard those spooky sounds. They said the noise from inside the old mill sounded like a dying man moaning and wailing. I guess it must have been weird."

Melissa gave Jan an inquiring look. "Maybe those kids just imagined they heard those weird sounds."

"Maybe," Jan replied, hastening her steps, "but I'd sure like to find out for myself, wouldn't you?"

Melissa hesitated.

"You aren't afraid, are you?"

"Of course not." Melissa tried to make her voice sound indifferent. "Ghosts! Who believes in them anyway?"

A half hour later, with the lunch Aunt Julie had packed for them, they went to the garage for the bikes.

"You can ride my new one," Jan offered generously. "I'll ride the small, older one."

As they peddled down the lane to the road, Melissa remembered Ed's promise to take her trail-riding today. How much more fun it would be riding Shadow through the woods to the old mill than this new ten-speed bike. But she kept her thoughts to herself.

They crossed the road and entered the woods by an old road that was grown up with grass so that the tire tracks were just barely visible. "This is part of the trail the Saddle Club takes during the trail rides," Jan informed her as they rode side by side on the uneven tire tracks. "They ride way back through the woods, then make a circle around by the old mill and take this road back to the Triple J."

The forest got denser the farther they went. The old road twisted through a grove of gloomy hemlocks, and Melissa began to feel uneasy as the trees closed in around them. She tried to tell herself that there were no such things as ghosts, but when she glanced up at the dark branches overhead, a little shiver traveled up the back of her neck. Not a shaft of sunlight shone through the green gloom, and even the wind hummed through the boughs in a low, hollow moan.

Neither girl talked. It was as though the somber hemlocks cast a spell of silence over them. There was only the muffled sound of their bicycle tires on the narrow, shadowy trail.

At last Melissa saw a break in the dark trees ahead and felt relieved that they were coming to a clearing. But her relief was short-lived, and her heart gave a thump when, through the heavy, layered green boughs, she caught a glimpse of an old stone building.

"That's the mill!" Jan whispered.

They stopped at the edge of the hemlocks and stared at the old gristmill that now loomed up before them. It did have a grim, desolate look about it, Melissa thought, as though it really could be haunted.

It stood aloof and mysterious, its old walls silently crumbling. The roof of gray, weathered cedar shakes sagged badly in the middle, and there was no glass left in the windows. Only dark square openings gaped at them like sightless eyes. Thick vines had taken over long ago, clutching the gray walls like an enormous green claw. An ancient oak in the mill yard threw deep gloom over the entire place.

Jan pointed to the enormous old waterwheel that stood on the other side of the mill by a dammed-up stream. "In the old days water from the millpond poured over a high dam and through the millrace causing the wheel to turn," she explained. "But now the sluice is dry."

Melissa stared at the wheel that stood gaunt and useless, like a silent ghost.

They ventured to the edge of the mill yard and sat forward on their bike seats to wait and to listen. After several long minutes Melissa whispered, "I don't hear any ghost."

"Let's ride closer and make sure," Jan said, her voice sounding braver than she really felt.

They rode across the mill yard, and when they came close to the stone side of the building, they stood up on their bike peddles to peer through a broken window. A wave of damp, musty air wafted over them from the inside, and at first they couldn't see a thing. Then gradually their eyes became adjusted to the dim interior, and they could make out the shadowy outline of the huge grain hopper that loomed above the round grindstone and what remained of the grain chutes that stretched down from the ceiling to the hopper like long ghostly arms. White-dusted cobwebs shimmered down the rafters in the eerie grayness. A heavy silence hung over everything.

As they were peering into the half-light of the old mill, a cloud passed over the sun and a breeze sprang up. It rippled the smooth waters of the millpond and rattled the leaves of the ancient oak.

Melissa and Jan sat very still, scarcely breathing, listening to another sound far inside the shadows of the old mill. A faint whisper of a sound it was. Like a ghost's moan?

Melissa felt her legs stiffen against the peddles of her bike. Jan's face turned so white that the freckles covering her nose stood out like brown polka dots. The moaning that had started out as a low whisper swelled in volume, growing louder and louder until it reached a shrill, spine-chilling shriek. It filled the dark recesses of the deserted old building like the anguished cry of a dying man.

"The ghost!" gasped Melissa. But that was impossible! Before she had time to think, the moaning and shrieking started up again, echoing across the mill yard like the wail of a banshee. Melissa's blood froze in her veins.

Jan's voice came out in a terrified squeal. "Let's get out of here!"

In an instant they had their bikes turned and were peddling at full speed across the mill yard to the safety of the woods. The dark hemlocks that had seemed so foreboding just a short while ago now closed their great boughs around them like sheltering arms. Even the winding, shadowy forest road, so difficult to follow, seemed to urge them on.

They pumped their peddles as fast as they could. Neither girl dared to look back over her shoulder, for the ghostly wail still echoed behind them. It seemed to be following them through the sunless forest like a menacing ogre, ready to catch up with them at any moment.

Nothing Has Changed

They rode without stopping until the dark hemlocks were well behind them. When the trees gave way to a small glade, they stopped to catch their breath.

"Let's eat our lunch here," Jan suggested, glancing around the sunny clearing.

While they munched potato chips and ham sandwiches, Melissa found herself asking, "We did hear those awful sounds, didn't we?"

Jan nodded and rolled her eyes. "You better believe it! Didn't they sound just like the moaning of a dying man? And that horrible wail!"

"But ghosts—" Melissa tried to reason with a puzzled shrug. "There are no such things!"

"Well, somebody, some*thing* was in that old mill, making those sounds," Jan declared, and at her words a cold shiver ran through Melissa.

Jan threw her a quick look. "Let's not tell Mom or Dad or Ed about it, though. They'd only laugh at us. They'd say there's nothing to be afraid of, and we just imagined the whole thing."

"I know," Melissa agreed. "Grown-ups are like that. Gran is always saying I'm just imagining things."

"We'll keep it a secret," said Jan. "Just between ourselves." She reached out, took Melissa's hand in hers and squeezed it to make the secret binding.

A sudden warmth filled Melissa. It would be fun having a secret to share with Jan. It would be almost like being best friends again.

They finished their lunch and peddled back to the Triple J. For the rest of the day, whenever they were alone, they talked about the haunted mill. Even though they had been frightened nearly out of their wits, they both had to agree that hearing those ghostly sounds had been exciting, and it was fun to have a secret to share.

That evening at dinner, though, Melissa forgot about the haunted mill when she sensed an air of excitement as Uncle Jeff and Ed took their places at the table.

"Do you know what the day after tomorrow is?" Uncle Jeff asked as he passed the girls the mashed potatoes.

"Sure, it's Saturday," answered Jan. "That's what it is."

"It's something else too," Ed reminded them, his eyes crinkling. "It's the gymkhana."

The next morning everybody was up bright and early at the Triple J. The entire day was full of preparations for the coming event. The girls helped Aunt Julie prepare for the picnic that would follow the trail ride. They helped Uncle Jeff and Ed set up barrels in the corral for the barrel race. They spent a long time in the stable grooming Shadow and Patches.

They took turns with the currycomb and the body brush. They cleaned the frog and sole of each hoof with a hoof pick and combed the tangles out of each tail and mane. By the time they were finished, Shadow and Patches looked like two fancy show horses.

Ed sauntered into the barn and eyed them. "A body'd think those two were going to the fair tomorrow, the way you've dandied them up," he teased, but there was approval in his voice as he ran his hand over the shining coats of the two groomed horses.

After he inspected each horse carefully, he turned his attention to Melissa. "Now how about practicing your gaits," he told her. "I think I can spare a few moments."

He glanced down disapprovingly at her blue sneakers. "There's an extra pair of Julie's boots in the tack room that I think will fit you, Missy.

You're going to do some real riding today, and you'll need them."

Melissa felt bright and happy as she made her way to the tack room for the boots. Ed had said that she was going to do some real riding today, and she could hardly wait to mount Shadow. She found the extra pair of boots and was glad Aunt Julie's feet were so small. The boots fit perfectly.

After Shadow was bridled and saddled, Melissa led her to the mounting block and swung into the saddle. Ed mounted his own gray stallion, and while they walked their mounts around the corral together to limber them up, he showed Melissa how to squeeze her knees gently against Shadow's sides and how to relax the reins to make her horse lope in an easy, rocking gait.

After Melissa had loped around the corral several times and Ed was satisfied with her gait, he taught her how to grip the saddle tightly with her legs, to ease up on the reins but at the same time to keep a firm feel of the bit in Shadow's mouth.

Melissa did as Ed instructed, and before she knew it, Shadow was throwing her long, slender legs out in front of her, her hooves pounding the turf in a sharp, quick tattoo as she went faster and faster around the corral. They were galloping, the wind rushing against Melissa's cheeks and a thrill of joy and freedom racing with her. It was more wonderful than she had ever imagined!

"Now that's real riding, isn't it?" Ed called

after her, his face beaming with approval. He watched her gallop around the corral several times, then motioned for her to stop.

"Now that you know how to walk, jog, lope, and gallop your horse, maybe you'd like to try putting Shadow through her paces," he said. "Just line her up there at the fence, and we'll see how you do."

Melissa felt a warm glow of pride as she rode Shadow to the far end of the corral, where Jan stood watching. Ed told her to circle the corral in a walk; then he called out the different gaits, mixing them up: "Lope, reverse, stop, back up, stop, reverse, lope, walk, gallop, jog."

Most of the time Melissa got mixed up, and Shadow's gait was wrong. But the little mare was responsive and alert, and the more Melissa practiced breaking her gait, the easier it became.

When Ed decided that she had practiced enough, he motioned for her to rein in her mount. He reached out for the lines to steady the sorrel while he talked. "You're doing some mighty fine riding for a beginner, Missy. Why, I reckon you and Shadow could ride in the gymkhana tomorrow, and I'm going to tell Jeff that you're all set for the trail ride. How would you like that?"

How would she like it! Melissa's joy knew no bounds. She had been hoping there would be some way that she and Shadow could be in the gymkhana.

She reached over in her saddle and blissfully

gave the sorrel a pat. "Do you really think we could, Ed?"

He nodded his answer with an encouraging wink, then swung his gray stallion around and rode off toward the high pasture, still smiling to himself.

With happy anticipation Melissa turned to Jan. She had expected Jan to be as excited and as glad as she. She was surprised to glimpse a frown of disapproval flicker briefly across the girl's face. Jan didn't say a word, but her mouth was drawn in a thin line, and she had that same funny look she'd had after Audrey's visit.

Melissa studied her with bafflement. Yesterday, on their bike ride to the old mill, things had seemed just great between them. They even had a secret to share. Now Jan was acting strange again.

Melissa's eyes searched hers, asking plainly: *Don't you want me to ride Shadow in the gymkhana?*

Jan's gaze slid past her, as if to avoid the questioning look. Her face was grim, almost sad, and even though she didn't say anything, Melissa knew the answer. *She doesn't want me to ride in the gymkhana because she doesn't want me to spoil her day and let her friends know that a disadvantaged city girl can ride and she can't.*

Melissa's triumph of the morning vanished, and her joy turned to bitter disappointment as she watched Jan stalk off to the house.

106

Her heart pounding with sudden hurt and anger, Melissa turned Shadow's head toward the gate. Gripping the saddle tightly with her legs, she sent the sorrel galloping out of the corral.

Yesterday, in good faith, she had thought that she and Jan could be best friends again. Now she knew that nothing had changed. She knew they could never be best friends—not ever—if she rode Shadow in the gymkhana tomorrow.

She gripped the reins tighter in her hands and urged Shadow on, across the bottom pasture, through the gate, and up the trail leading to the waterfall.

Riding for Help

The day of the gymkhana dawned warm and clear with a bright blue canopy of sky stretching over fields and pastures. Along the lane leading to the horse barn, several cars were parked; their owners were in the corral saddling up their horses that were stabled at the Triple J. From her bedroom window Melissa watched Aunt Julie and Uncle Jeff join the others and set off on the trail ride. They were to meet the remaining members of the Saddle Club at the start of the trail, about a mile down the road from the Triple J ranch.

Of course, Aunt Julie and Uncle Jeff had expected Melissa to be with them on the ride, and

108

when she had told them that she was not going, a surprised Aunt Julie had exclaimed, "Not going! Why, honey, you don't want to miss the trail ride. It's one of the nicest things about the gymkhana."

Melissa had turned away from Aunt Julie's pleading eyes and glanced down at her folded hands. "I—I promised Mama I'd write her a letter," she had replied lamely, "and I haven't done it yet."

She had wished Aunt Julie and Uncle Jeff would understand and leave her alone. But Uncle Jeff had persisted, "Ed said you wanted to ride in the trail ride, Missy. You can write your letter another time. Today is the gymkhana—fun day!"

A little worry-wrinkle had appeared between Aunt Julie's eyes. "You aren't ill, dear, are you?"

Melissa had shaken her head. "Oh, no. I'm all right. Honest."

Finally they had given in and insisted no more. With a look of concern and bewilderment still in her eyes, Aunt Julie had lingered to tell Melissa that they wouldn't be gone long, only a couple of hours. Ed and Jan would be around if she wanted anything. Then Aunt Julie had given Melissa's hand a squeeze and hurried to join Uncle Jeff.

Now as they rode off, they looked so festive—Aunt Julie mounted on her beautiful bay and Uncle Jeff riding his big roan. As she watched them go, Melissa couldn't help wishing that she and Shadow were riding with them.

She turned from the window and propped herself up on the bed to start her letter. She would tell Mama and Gran everything that had happened, that it had been a big mistake to come here.

As she was thinking of what to write, her eyes wandered from the letter to the china horse, which she had placed on the dressing table. There, alone against the mirror, its tiny black hooves spread apart as though it were trotting, it looked more like Shadow than it had in the store.

No, she decided, thinking of the beautiful sorrel in the pasture below, it wasn't a mistake that she had come to the Triple J, now that she had learned to ride and to love Shadow. It was just that things hadn't worked out between her and Jan. Mama and Gran would understand.

Or would they? Melissa nibbled the end of her pencil and stared down at the blank sheet of writing paper. Would Mama and Gran really understand what Jan felt about her? Had she herself understood? Gran said many times that not understanding one another often leads to fear. And fear leads to hard feelings.

Her fingers tightened around the pencil as she wrote the words "Dear Mama and Gran." She wrote the letters slowly and carefully as if she didn't want to finish them and go on with the rest of the letter. She tried to think of what else to write, but words escaped her. Her eyes wandered to the window, and she stared idly at the deserted corral. Set up with props for the gymkhana, it reminded her of an empty stage before a performance.

All at once the emptiness of the house closed in around her. She sat for a long time listening to the ticking of the grandfather clock in the hallway. *Tick-tock-tick-tock.* It sounded as lonesome as she felt, and suddenly she knew that she couldn't stay in this big silent house a minute longer.

She pushed her letter aside. She would write to Mama and Gran another time. Meanwhile she'd ride Shadow until the others got back.

She hurried across the room, went out into the hall, and down the backstairs. She let the kitchen door slam quickly behind her in her eagerness to get away from the empty house. She crossed the side yard to look for the sorrel, but Shadow wasn't at her usual place in the bottom pasture. Then she remembered that Ed had moved the Triple J horses to the high pasture so that the Saddle Club could keep their mounts here. She was about to hike up to the high pasture when strange sounds in the horse barn made her pause by the corral gate to listen.

There they were again, a loud snorting noise and the dull thump of hooves. Puzzled, Melissa stepped inside the stable. She paused again, listening. The sounds seemed to come from Princess' stall. The next moment she glimpsed Jan standing in front of the stall, staring wide-eyed and frightened at the beautiful Arabian mare.

"What's the matter?" Melissa called, hurrying up to the stall to stand beside Jan. Beyond the gate the big silver-gray horse was pacing back and forth and pawing the floor with her hooves.

"I think she's about ready to have her foal," Jan said, an odd note of worry in her voice, "and there's no one around." She turned to look at Melissa, and Melissa could see that she was frightened—thoroughly, helplessly frightened.

"Where's Ed?"

"I don't know," Jan replied with a puzzled shake of her head. "He always stays here during the trail ride to get last-minute things ready for the gymkhana. But he's nowhere around now. I called and called. I even went to the tack room and to his trailer."

Melissa thought about the high pasture, to which Ed had moved the horses, and her eyes brightened. "Maybe he's with the horses in the high pasture."

"He could be," Jan said with relief. "Let's go and find out." And without saying anything more she fled from the barn with Melissa at her heels.

They scrambled through the bars of the corral

With sinking hearts they stared down at the spot where the tire tracks had worn away the grass. The truck was gone. Ed must be off somewhere and Frieda with him.

gate, barely avoiding collision with a gray tabby cat that was mousing in the tall grass by the fence. Half running, they made their way up the gentle slope. When they reached the hilltop, their eyes swept quickly over the pasture, but they saw only the Triple J horses. Ed's gray was among them, but they couldn't find Ed anywhere.

Grazing by the fence, Patches looked up curiously as the girls approached. Jan ran and threw her arms around the pinto's neck. "Where's Ed?" she moaned.

Patches mumbled low in her throat, flicked her ears, and gave Jan a playful nip.

The girls' gaze surveyed the pasture again in one last, desperate sweep; then they turned and started down the trail, Patches and Shadow following.

There was one more place to look. Jan led the way around the back of the barns, where Ed always parked his pickup, hoping to find the old red truck standing there. With sinking hearts they stared down at the spot where the tire tracks had worn away the grass. The truck was gone. Now they knew for certain that Ed must be off somewhere and Frieda with him.

"He must have forgotten something for the gymkhana and drove into town," Jan said miserably. "Who knows when he'll be back."

Her eyes had a desperate look in them as they lifted to the long, empty lane, and Melissa knew what she was thinking. What if Ed didn't return in time? What if Princess lost her foal because there was nobody here who knew how to help?

A shrill whinny drew them like a magnet to the mare's stall. Princess gazed at them with a wild, frightened look, her deep brown eyes glassy like shiny marbles. Her delicate nostrils flared in and out as she started pacing and pawing again.

"If she keeps that up, she might harm the foal," Jan said. "I wonder what Ed would do if he were here." Instinctively, she began to talk softly to the horse. "There, girl. Quiet, girl. Whoa there, Princess."

Her words did seem to help a little, and with more gentle urging the mare stopped pacing and stood panting, her full sides heaving convulsively. She was quiet now, but how long would she remain this way?

Melissa's hands trembled as she clutched the stall gate. Princess needed help and she needed it right now. If there were only *something* they could do!

She blinked hard as she tried to think. She remembered Gran telling her that when trouble comes and you don't know what to do, it helps to say a prayer. Melissa squeezed her eyes tightly shut. "Please, God," she murmured, "help Princess."

She opened her eyes, and something clicked suddenly in her brain. It was such a simple, obvious solution that she wondered why they

115

hadn't thought of it before. She blurted out her idea with a burst of confidence. "Let's call the vet!"

"Don't you think I didn't think of that?" Jan snapped with impatience, but Melissa knew that the sharpness of her words was caused by fear. "Doc Harmon, the vet, is a member of the Saddle Club, and he's on the trail ride. He was going to look in at Princess when he got here for the gymkhana."

"Couldn't we ride to get him?" Melissa suggested eagerly. "You know, we could ride up the woods road past the mill and meet the Saddle Club on their way back."

Jan shook her head. "The woods road ends at the mill, and the trail past it is too rough for bikes. Only hikers and horses can travel it."

"Then there's only one thing we can do," Melissa ventured boldly. "We'll have to tack up Shadow and Patches and ride after them."

Jan looked at her with large, frightened eyes. "But what about me?" she shrilled. "I couldn't ride Patches."

Melissa set her mouth firmly. "You got to. I couldn't find my way back in those woods by myself."

"Are you crazy!" piped Jan.

Melissa let out a long sigh and thought a moment, her lip caught between her teeth. With a sudden flash of insight she said, "You ride Shadow and I'll ride Patches. Oh, Jan, Shadow is so gentle and patient. She wouldn't throw you."

"I couldn't! I couldn't! Can't you understand that!" The words burst from Jan in something like terror.

Melissa stared at her incredulously. She'd had no idea how deep Jan's fear was. "Jan," she said in an even voice, "when I'm afraid, I think of God and that he's always with me. He'll be with you too."

"He wasn't with me when I fell off my horse the first time," Jan snapped back. "You're stupid—that's what you are. Stupid, stupid, stupid!"

Melissa could feel a hot flush rise to her cheeks. "No, you are for acting so weird about riding—and about God. If you really believe that God is with you, he will be. But you have to believe. And about riding—you know Patches and love her. And you know all about her gaits. I bet you could ride her just swell, but you're too scared to do it and too stubborn to let God help you!"

Melissa stopped and drew in a deep breath, waiting for Jan's angry reply, but the girl just stared dully at her, as if she were in some kind of trance.

Melissa swung around toward the tack room. Anger and frustration sharpened her tone. "If you're so chicken that you won't help Princess, then you don't deserve her colt," she flung back over her shoulder. She could feel Jan's eyes bore through her, but she went on determinedly, "I just might be able to find the right trail myself!"

She was so upset that her hands were shaking as she got Shadow's gear, then hurried across the corral to let the sorrel through the gate. Shadow stood patiently by the mounting block while Melissa slipped the bit between her teeth and brought the bridle up over her head and ears. She was thankful now that Ed had taught her how to tack up.

Her hands still shook while she worked, but she kept talking to Shadow, explaining about Princess and how they had to get help as quickly as possible. She remembered that when Ed wanted the horses to stand still, he'd always talk softly to them. Ed had said that horses understand everything you tell them, and they'll never kick up a fuss if you explain things calmly. So she went on talking to Shadow.

"We're going to get Uncle Jeff," she said, checking the tack to make sure it was all right. "We're going to find him and the vet and bring them back here as fast as we can. And you're going to help me find them, Shadow."

Struggling with the heavy saddle, she finally got it into place and secured the cinch strap. Then she flung her legs over the sorrel's broad back and settled herself firmly in the saddle. With pounding heart she took the reins in her hands and urged Shadow out of the corral.

A shout came from the tack room just as she

was riding through the gate. She reined in the sorrel and looked back over her shoulder to see Jan leading Patches to the mounting block.

"Wait for me," called Jan. "If I have to ride, I'd rather ride Patches. She's my horse."

Melissa stared with unbelieving joy. "Oh, Jan," she shouted encouragement, "you can do it! I know you can!"

Jan drew in a very deep breath, and after an anxious moment she climbed the mounting block and swung into the saddle. When she walked Patches to the corral gate, she was pale around the lips but managed a wavery smile.

"Just don't go galloping down the lane," she said in a small, tight voice, "and—and I think I'll be okay."

Even so, Melissa noticed how white Jan's knuckles were as her hands gripped the reins. But she was relieved as she listened to Patches' easy walk behind her. The frisky pinto seemed to understand that she was carrying someone special, for her gait was as ladylike as Shadow's.

By the time they reached the forest road, Jan seemed to relax a bit and sat straighter in her saddle. She even urged Patches to a jog when they reached the hemlocks. It wasn't until Melissa glimpsed the old crumbling walls of the mill through the trees that a feeling of uneasiness began to creep over her again.

Would the ghost of Henry Dunbar be there to greet them today? she wondered. Would the ghost moan again? She didn't dare to think what Patches' reaction would be if it did.

Sitting stiff in the saddle, Melissa needed all the self-control she could muster to ride past the mill at an easy walk. But when at last they had passed it with only the muted sound of the horses' hoofbeats to break the silence of the woods, Melissa drew in a long breath. "Whew!" She went limp in the saddle and was relieved to let Jan take the lead.

The road had dwindled into a trail, unknown to Melissa, that wound through a heavily wooded area ahead. But Jan was riding with a new confidence now, as if she had ridden this trail many times before, and Melissa followed gratefully, allowing her thoughts to return to Princess. She hoped they wouldn't be too late and that the foal would be born safely. She knew how much that foal meant to Jan.

Up ahead the trail branched off and plunged into thick pines. All around them the forest was deep and silent. Melissa began to wonder whether Jan really did know the way, never having ridden the trail before. She raised herself in the saddle and called over Shadow's bobbing head, "Are we on the right trail?"

Would the ghost moan again? Sitting stiff in the saddle, Melissa needed all the self-control she could muster to ride past the mill at an easy walk.

Jan nodded and called back reassuringly, "Dad described it to me so many times that I know it by heart."

She kept Patches loping in an easy gait, and Melissa thought: *She rides like a pro. She must have put Patches through her gaits many times in her mind to be able to ride like this. Won't Uncle Jeff and Aunt Julie be surprised when they see her!*

But where was the Saddle Club, and how far would they have to ride to find them? The trail seemed endless as it wound across streams, past rocky ledges, and through stands of tall trees.

Melissa tried to become absorbed in the beauty of the big trees, the fresh spicy scent of pine needles spread out like a soft carpet on the forest floor, the glimpses of sky that shone like blue crystal through the treetops. It was a perfect day to be trail-riding, and her heart should be singing. But it wasn't. She kept thinking about the Arabian mare alone in her stall at the Triple J.

Suddenly Jan brought Patches to a slow walk and held up her hand. Then Melissa heard it—the echoing thud of hoofbeats coming down the trail toward them. As the hoofbeats came closer, the sound of jingling bridles and laughing voices further broke the empty silence of the surrounding forest.

"It's them!" Jan cried, and forgetting her fear, she sent Patches off on a fast gallop up the trail toward the riders.

Uncle Jeff's big roan came into view, and Patches raced to meet it.

"Dad," Jan cried, "it's Princess! She's ready to foal!"

But Uncle Jeff wasn't listening to what she was shouting. He reined in the roan and stared, unbelievingly, at his daughter. "Janny, you're riding!" he exclaimed. He swung off his mount and ran up to where Jan had brought Patches to a halt. He looked up at her, his eyes filled with hope and happiness. Melissa's heart gave a glad thump as she watched father and daughter.

"You're riding!" Uncle Jeff said again as if he still couldn't believe what he saw.

"I know," Jan said with a tremulous laugh, "but, Dad, I had to. And—and Missy made me. It was for Princess."

"What about Princess?" her father asked, his happy face sobering.

"She's foaling and she needs help real quick."

As she spoke, a gray-haired man with a black saddlebag nosed his mount out of the line of riders and went galloping down the trail toward the mill road.

Uncle Jeff mounted his roan. He paused just long enough to flash his daughter another quick, happy smile; then turning the roan's head toward the mill road, he galloped off after Doc Harmon.

Melissa felt weak with relief as she watched them go. She hoped it wouldn't be too late. She hoped they would get to Princess in time.

She watched until the trees closed around them; then she turned back to the others. For the first time she was aware of the line of faces staring at her and Jan. She saw Aunt Julie, with a happy smile for Jan but at the same time a worried look for Princess. She saw Audrey on her palomino gelding, the look of surprise still on her face as she stared at Jan mounted on Patches. The other riders were all strange to Melissa, but they were both smiling and anxious looking too.

Mr. Van Doren walked his mount to the head of the line of riders. "We'd better get back to the Triple J and see how things are turning out," he said. And at his command the Saddle Club followed him down the trail.

Audrey rode ahead with another girl, but Jan didn't seem to mind. She followed Aunt Julie's beautiful bay, and Melissa and Shadow were right behind them. Jan turned once in her saddle to smile reassuringly at Melissa.

"Everything's going to be all right," she called back, trying to make her voice sound confident. "It—it just has to be, Missy. After all, today's fun day!"

The Gymkhana

Ed and Frieda were waiting by the corral gate when the Saddle Club came riding up. Melissa's spirits lifted when she saw Ed's eyes shining and his smile reaching almost up to his ears. Nobody had to ask how Princess was. Everyone knew by the way Ed looked that now that Uncle Jeff and Doc Harmon were here, everything would be all right.

After they rode into the corral and reined in their mounts, Ed tried to explain everything. He and Frieda had gone to town to pick up one of the prizes Uncle Jeff had forgotten. He had checked in on Princess before he left, and everything had seemed to be all right. It was only after he got back and found Uncle Jeff and Doc Harmon in the stable that he knew something had gone wrong.

"I sure am glad two gals rustled up enough courage to ride after them," he added with a special wink for Melissa and Jan.

Now that everything was under control, Aunt Julie dismounted and called out, "Who's hungry?"

At a yell from the boys in the club, Ed said, "I guess everyone is, after all the excitement." He strode over to the big grill in the side yard and turned the meat that was roasting on a spit over red-hot coals. The tantalizing smells that came from the barbecue made the young people groan and rub their stomachs.

Aunt Julie sent the girls scurrying inside to help her with the rest of the meal. She hustled about the kitchen, checking on the barbecue sauce that had been left simmering in a large kettle on the stove and opening the refrigerator to take out the tossed salad. She handed the salad bowl to Jan and a platter of rolls to Melissa to carry outside to the long picnic table.

Once they were outside and alone, Jan turned to Melissa with a look of gratitude in her blue eyes. "It's great what you did today, Missy, to help Princess," she said. "Especially when it's not your foal that's in trouble. Most other kids couldn't have cared less."

Melissa sank down on one of the benches and

smiled weakly at Jan. "Then you're not mad at me for all those things I said in the barn?"

Jan shook her head. "I deserved every word. You're really the best friend I ever had, Missy."

She paused a moment, then said, "You know, you were right about God. When there was nothing left for me to do but to trust in him, he overcame my terrible fear of riding. God was with me on that ride, Missy. I know he was!"

Their eyes met and a sudden light of awareness and understanding shone in their steady gaze. Jan wasn't afraid anymore. And neither was Melissa afraid of not being liked for herself. They had shown each other that they could overcome their fears, and through this awareness they had both grown to know one another.

"Thanks, God," Melissa said in silent prayer.

The next moment she jumped up from the picnic bench, her face full of smiles, and asked, "Are you going to ride Patches in the gymkhana?"

Jan nodded and laughed. "We'll both ride in the egg race, Missy, even if it means scrambled eggs!"

Aunt Julie came out of the kitchen to talk to Ed; a minute later he rang the big brass dinner bell in the yard, and the hungry riders gathered around the grill for the barbecue.

They were just finishing the meal when Uncle Jeff and Doc Harmon came out of the stable. An expectant hush settled over the gathering as they watched the two men walk across the corral and into the yard.

Melissa's heart quickened, and Jan's eyes were round with suspense. It seemed an eternity before either man said anything. Then Doc Harmon announced that Princess had a colt. "Mother and son are doing fine," he assured them.

Everybody hooted and clapped, and above the din Jan's voice rose eagerly. "Can we see the foal?"

Uncle Jeff shook his head. "Better wait a while, Janny. He's newborn and still skittish. Time enough to see him after the gymkhana."

Aunt Julie handed the two men plates piled with food, and while they ate, the grown-ups sat in the yard and talked as they drank cups of Ed's specially brewed coffee.

The young people congregated by the corral gate and sipped ice-cold lemonade. They asked Jan and Melissa to tell about their exciting ride for help.

Jan told about finding Princess, about their desperate search for Ed, and then how with Melissa's help she had gotten up the courage to ride Patches.

"Good for you!" a boy named Kevin broke in, giving her a pat on the shoulder.

Not the center of attention, Audrey stood off from the others and busied herself brushing down Silver Beauty's shining, gold-colored coat. But once in a while she turned her head in Jan's direction, and when she did, Melissa noticed that there was a little corner-of-the-mouth smile for her friend.

After they had gone through every detail of their exciting ride, Kevin's older brother, Hal, spoke up in a teasing voice. "Did you hear the ghost when you rode past the mill? Old Kevin here claims he and his gang have."

"If you don't believe in ghosts, you should ride out to the mill yourself sometime, Hal," Kevin returned curtly. "Then you'll find out!"

The older boy grinned in a superior manner. "You young 'uns sure get a charge out of things," he said and swaggered off to look after his horse.

Kevin snorted. "Hal thinks he's super-cool and knows everything there is to know now that he's turned sixteen, but I was with the kids from school who hiked out there, and, wow, did we hear those weird sounds!"

"I wonder what causes them," asked Gail, the girl with whom Audrey had ridden back to the Triple J. "There can't really be a ghost at the old mill, can there?"

"Are you kidding!" Kevin exploded.

A lengthy discussion followed, with a few arguments as to whether or not the old mill really was haunted. They talked on about it until the dinner bell rang again, this time to announce the start of the games. Jan crooked her arm through Melissa's, and they walked off with the others to watch the contests.

As they stood together by the corral fence and waited for the games to begin, both girls stole longing glances at the barn where Princess and her foal were. They could hardly wait to see the new baby colt. But the riders were sorting out their horses in the bottom pasture and riding to the corral, bridles jingling and saddle leather creaking. Uncle Jeff used the bullhorn to announce the first event. Soon the girls became lost in the fun and thrills of the gymkhana.

The first contest, the barrel race, was exciting to watch as the contestants wove a course in and out among the barrels set up in the corral. It wasn't easy to guide a horse through the line of barrels without knocking one down. Hal, the winner, received a new halter as the prize. He was so proud of himself that he rode around the corral, holding up the halter for everyone to see.

After the barrel race Uncle Jeff announced the ribbon race for the women. Melissa and Jan cheered Aunt Julie as she and her partner held a ribbon of crepe paper without tearing it while going through the different gaits together on their horses. The prize was a set of brushes.

The pickup, or rescue race, was the most exciting. The men lined up their horses at one end of the corral while the women to be "rescued" stood at the opposite end. At the signal each horse and rider galloped across the corral. The women grabbed the arms of their partners and quickly swung onto the horses as they circled a barrel and galloped for the finish line. The winners, Mr. and Mrs. Van Doren, received brand-new lead ropes.

The boot race was the funniest. The contestants had to take off their boots and mix them up at the far end of the corral. Then they walked back to the gate and mounted their horses. At the signal they raced for the pile of boots, searched for their own, and rode back with them. Everybody laughed as they watched Ed scramble for his boots, only to ride back with Mrs. Van Doren's.

Other events followed: the flag race, the jumping contest, the back-up race, the pony express ride, and the break-your-gait-or-out race. The last event was the egg race.

Melissa mounted Shadow at the starting line next to Jan and Patches, and Ed gave both of the girls an encouraging wink when he handed them spoons with an egg balanced on each. As Uncle Jeff called out the gaits, Melissa tried to hold her spoon steady. Everything went smoothly while she was walking Shadow around the corral. But when she had to jog, off went the egg. It was Jan's egg which stayed on the spoon the longest.

Melissa felt a tingle of joy at the fact that Jan had won. Jan's face was flushed with happiness when Dick Braum, one of the contest judges, handed her a new pair of reins for Patches. Then her eyes grew misty as everyone clapped and gathered around her. Even Audrey rode up on

Silver Beauty to congratulate her. "Janny, I had no *idea* you could ride like that," she said.

Jan flushed modestly. "It was really Patches who went through the gaits," she said, reaching over to give the saucy little mare a pat on her flanks. "Silver Beauty is probably a lot faster."

"Yes, but she's still a frisky two-year-old," Audrey said with a sigh. "Dad says she needs a lot more training to get her over her coltish ways." With a slow smile for Melissa she said, "For a city girl you sure are learning fast, Missy."

Melissa smiled back, taking what Audrey had said as a compliment.

Finally, Uncle Jeff picked up his bullhorn, and an expectant hush fell over the corral. "The races are over, but we have one more prize," he called out to the riders. "This prize is to go to the best sport in   gymkhana, and I suggest this year we give it to the rider who made our fun day a really happy one."

Melissa held her breath, wondering who the winner would be. When she heard her own name called, she could hardly believe her ears. Even when Jan gave her a little push to ride up to accept the prize, she could scarcely believe it was really hers.

Uncle Jeff held out a beautiful new saddle blanket, and amid the "oh's" and "ah's" that came from the other riders, Melissa couldn't help feeling a little overwhelmed. Her heart raced and

132

her hands shook. She knew her riding wasn't good enough to warrant such a wonderful prize. But when she glanced up at Uncle Jeff, and his smile told her that being the best sport in the gymkhana was every bit as important as winning any of the events, she returned his smile—with pride shining in her eyes—and accepted the blanket.

Everybody was clapping as she rode back to the gate. Amid all the applause Melissa hugged the blanket close to her. If only Mama and Gran were here to see her! How happy and proud they would be—as happy and as proud of her as Jan and Uncle Jeff and Aunt Julie and Ed were right now.

Ghost Sounds Again

"I'd say this was the best gymkhana ever," Uncle Jeff announced when everybody had left and they were helping Ed unsaddle the horses.

"It certainly was the most exciting one," Aunt Julie declared. "Who would have ever dreamed that Princess would have her foal the day of the gymkhana!"

Melissa and Jan couldn't hold back their desire any longer. In one voice they begged, "Can we see the foal now?"

"I don't see why not," Uncle Jeff replied. "Come along, but don't make too much noise. As I told you before, the young thing's still skittish."

In awe and wonder they all but tiptoed into the

stable, Frieda following on soft padded paws. From Princess' stall came a gentle rustle in the straw, and when the girls peered over the gate, they saw a sight that made them let out their breath in a long happy sigh. *"Oh-h-h!"*

Lying curled on the clean straw was a tiny horse with a small, white, diamond-shaped star between his two bright eyes. His velvet coat, silver-gray like his mother's, was soft and new-looking. His small, pointed ears twitched forward, and he quivered all over when he sensed the girls' presence. Princess stood at her foal's side, her long, graceful neck arched down as she watched over him.

"Isn't he beautiful?" murmured Jan.

"Uh-huh!" breathed Melissa. "And so tiny. Will he ever grow to be as big as Princess?"

"He sure will," replied Uncle Jeff, "and it won't be long until he's prancing around the pasture with his mother."

Melissa felt Uncle Jeff's arm close around her. "We are grateful for what you and Jan did today, Missy," he said. "If you girls hadn't warned us about Princess, and if Doc and I hadn't arrived as soon as we did, this little colt wouldn't be alive now."

Melissa stared in awe at the foal. If it hadn't been for her and Jan, Uncle Jeff had said.... Something strange and wonderful stirred inside her.

"Dad," Jan spoke and Melissa could feel the

135

warmth in her voice, "I want this to be Missy's foal as well as mine, and when she comes again next summer, she can help train it."

Uncle Jeff turned to Melissa; his eyes, crinkly at the corners, were smiling down at her. "What do you say to that, Missy?" he asked.

Melissa couldn't find the words. She was so surprised and happy that Jan wanted to share the foal with her that she could only nod and smile in answer to Uncle Jeff's question.

Jan said, "We have to think of a name for our foal, Missy. What shall we call him?"

They stopped talking to think. Melissa tried to recall all the horses' names she had ever heard, but none of them seemed to fit this cute little colt.

It was Aunt Julie's quiet voice that broke the long silence. "Look," she whispered, "the foal's getting up!"

As they watched the little horse struggle up on his long, wobbly legs, Melissa felt that she just had to open the stall gate and help him. But he managed by himself, and at last he was standing on all four legs, swaying a little but with a cocky expression that made them all laugh out loud. Princess prodded him gently with her muzzle. He

When Jan and Melissa peered over the gate, they saw a sight that made them let out their breath in a long happy sigh. Lying curled on the clean straw was a tiny new horse.

stretched out his nose to find his supper, and his little black curly tail twitched back and forth with pleasure. He seemed so happy and pleased with himself that Melissa knew at once what she would like to call him.

"Let's call him Happy!" she exclaimed.

Jan rolled her eyes thoughtfully. "Happy—" she murmured. Then, with a gleam of laughter in her eyes, she piped, "Hey, that's a neat name, isn't it, Dad?"

"It sure is," Uncle Jeff replied. "I couldn't think of a better one for that spunky little fellow."

"We'd better leave Happy to his supper and get our own," Aunt Julie said finally. "It's getting late."

Reluctantly they pulled themselves away from the stall, and it wasn't until the next day, after church and Sunday dinner, that they were able to see Happy again. After hurriedly changing out of their Sunday dresses and into jeans and shirts, they raced each other to the horse barn. Melissa was the first to arrive at Princess' stall. She peered up over the stall gate, and when she didn't see Princess or Happy, she cried, "It's empty!"

"They must be outside," Jan said. "Ed probably has them in the bottom pasture."

They turned and ran out of the stable and across the corral, almost bumping into Ed, who was saddling his gray.

"Whoa there a minute!" he called after them, lifting the saddle over his horse but posing with it in midair as they flew by. "Where are you two galloping off to? You have a caller. Audrey rode over to see your new colt. She's down in the pasture right now waiting for you."

"That's where we're going," Jan flung back, following Melissa in her crooked run.

Crossing the lane, they couldn't resist calling at once to Audrey. In the same breath they shouted, "His name's Happy."

"Missy named him," Jan informed Audrey when they reached the pasture. "He's her colt too."

"You mean you're going to *share* him?" Audrey asked, blinking her eyes unbelievingly.

Melissa was taken aback by the blunt remark, but then, she thought, maybe it was just Audrey's natural reaction to blurt that out. Maybe Audrey never had anyone to share things with. Oh, she had lots of friends, being the most popular girl in school. But did she really have a *best* friend, one whom she understood and who understood her, a friend to share things with?

At that moment Melissa found herself feeling sorry for the girl who seemed to have everything.

After the three of them had admiringly watched the little colt for a while, Jan said, "Let's trail-ride in the woods."

Audrey looked surprised. "Well, okay, but I brought my swimsuit. I thought you'd rather go swimming."

"Not today," Jan said with a twinkle for Melissa. "I have a lot of riding to catch up on."

Audrey mounted Silver Beauty and followed Melissa and Jan back to the corral. After Shadow and Patches were saddled, all three jogged down the lane in the direction of the forest road.

As they entered the woods, Audrey turned, her eyes sparkling with excitement. "I know where we can go. Let's ride to the gristmill."

Melissa and Jan looked at one another with surprise. "Why do you want to ride all the way out there?" Jan asked. "You've ridden past that old mill lots of times."

"I know, but only on trail rides," replied Audrey. "We never stopped to listen and find out if there really were those weird sounds. Anyway, if there are, I don't believe a ghost makes them."

"We don't believe in ghosts, either," Melissa said resolutely, "but lots of people have heard those spooky sounds."

"Maybe they have," Audrey challenged, "but they have never tried to find out what makes them. Wouldn't you like to know?"

"Okay, let's go," Jan spoke up with a meaningful glance at Melissa. Catching the bright look in Jan's eyes, Melissa knew what she was thinking. It would be fun to see Audrey's reaction when she heard those weird sounds.

Impatient to be off, Silver Beauty surged ahead; Shadow and Patches followed at a more leisurely gait. Frieda trailed after them, darting through the bushes now and then to sniff out a rabbit trail or to peer up into a hollow tree where a gray squirrel scampered to escape notice. But when they entered the dark grove of hemlocks, she kept to the trail, trotting close to the hooves of Jan's pinto.

As they came nearer to the old mill, Melissa's enthusiasm for ghost hunting began to wane, and she felt her old fear returning. She knew it was silly to feel like this, with Audrey riding so confidently in the lead, but she couldn't help herself. And she knew by the way Jan sat stiff in her saddle that she was experiencing the same feeling.

When they rode out of the hemlocks and came within sight of the mill, they dismounted and looped their reins around some stout tree trunks along the edge of the woods. Jan helped Melissa tie a good bowline knot that would hold Shadow if she should get frightened and try to run.

Audrey took the lead as they started across the mill yard. They had gone only halfway across when the low, ghostly moan greeted them.

Jan gave Melissa a knowing look and said in a hushed voice, "There's our ghost. It knows we're coming."

Melissa wondered how Jan could talk so lightly at a time like this, but when she saw the stunned expression on Audrey's face, she felt like giggling in spite of her nervousness.

Jan spoke again, with a little note of I-told-you-so in her voice. "Now you know the ghostly sounds are for real, Audrey."

The girl regained her composure and brought up her chin in a defiant tilt. "I didn't say they weren't real," she retorted. "All I said was, we're going to find out what makes them."

The moaning stopped. Her confidence restored, Audrey urged them the rest of the way across the mill yard. But when they approached the mill itself, Melissa could see her steps lagging.

They paused again to listen. In the silence that followed, Jan said, "There's no use standing here. Listening will only make us more scared." And taking a long breath, she marched up to the old wooden door. She lifted the ancient latch, and the door with its weathered gray boards creaked painfully open. Huddled closely together, the three girls stepped cautiously into the dim, musty interior.

Melissa glanced back over her shoulder at the sunny doorway. "Come on, Frieda. Come on, girl," she coaxed.

The dog, which had followed them up to the mill, now sat on the stone doorstep and whined her protests as she watched them fade into the shadows of the dimly lighted room. Despite Melissa's whistles she wouldn't come in. "Smart dog!" thought Melsisa as she turned to follow Jan and Audrey farther into the gloomy old building.

Instinctively they moved toward a shaft of sunlight coming through one of the broken windows. The dim light revealed the dark outlines of the roof timbers overhead and cast a pale glow on the long shadowy chutes leading down from the timbers to the huge hopper above the millstone. Dust motes danced around the girls as they crept forward. Just before they reached the hopper, a bat flew out and flapped its way toward the open door.

Audrey shrieked and backed into a huge cobweb. With a choked cry Melissa followed her. "Yuch!" they both muttered, fighting their way through the sticky threads.

They were still struggling with the web when the low moaning suddenly rose to a deafening wail. They felt trapped and about ready to panic when Jan took their hands firmly in hers and guided them past the web. When the wail subsided to a low moan again, she said, trying to keep her voice matter-of-fact and steady, "This must have been the grinding room."

"Wh-who cares what it was?" moaned Audrey. "Let's get out of here."

Jan paused to look full at her friend. She asked, "You wanted to find out what makes the creepy sounds, didn't you? Well, we're here now so let's find out."

Without protesting further, Audrey followed as Jan led the way to the millstone and the grain chutes that had poured the grain from the storage bin above down to the hopper and from there onto the grindstone. Although many years had passed since the millstone had been used to grind wheat into flour, a faint musty odor of grain still lingered in the dusty air, and the floor-boards still shone silvery smooth with flour dust, giving the place a ghostly appearance.

Jan bent to examine the hopper, but Melissa and Audrey stepped back, putting their hands over their hair. They had no desire to encounter any more bats.

"Nothing here that could make that noise," Jan said finally. She straightened up and looked around her. "Let's stand real still and listen. Maybe if we listen hard enough and think hard enough, we can figure out where the moaning and wailing sound comes from."

It seemed like a good idea, and for the moment the girls forgot their fright and concentrated on listening. But as they stood quietly, straining their ears, the moaning stopped as abruptly and as unexpectedly as it had started, and a silence as foreboding as the dim interior of the mill itself, hung over them.

Melissa didn't feel any braver in the eerie quiet. It was as if the ghost, realizing that its wails had not frightened them away, were just holding its breath and watching them from the gloomy shadows. She almost wished the weird moaning would start up again.

But when it did, sounding louder and creepier than ever, cold chills seized all three of them, and they stood rigid against the big hopper, having to force themselves to stay and listen.

When at last the moaning subsided, Jan stam-

144

• jesus •

Sonrise Creations 1984© micki 380023

Stories of the Bible ACTIVITY STICKERS

Jesus

"And she shall bring forth a son, and thou shalt call His name JESUS: for He shall save His people from their sins."

Story from Matthew 1:21 (KJV)

Sonrise Creations inc.

P.O. Box 1731
Grand Rapids, MI 49501

illustrated by: micki shugars

mered brokenly, "It—it doesn't seem to be coming from anywhere around here."

"It sounds as if it might be coming from over there," Melissa said, pointing with a shaky hand to a window-shaped opening at the far side of the room.

"It does at that," Audrey agreed, a flush of excitement on her cheeks. "Come on, let's find out."

They crept past the shadows of the hopper and made their way across the room until at last they reached the opening in the far wall. Standing on tiptoe, Jan stuck her head through the broken window, and the other two girls peered out also.

They were puzzled, all wondering the same thing, as they stared across the empty millrace to the millpond. Why had the ghostly sound led them here? Below them was only the skeletal frame of the waterwheel, which had long stood motionless, its wooden paddles warped and gray.

They lingered for a moment by the window, drawing in deep breaths of fresh air. It was good to see daylight again, to inhale the spicy aroma of the pines on the other side of the millpond, to feel warm sun.

A breeze rippled across the pond and brushed their faces like a soft, cool hand. At the same time it hummed through the warped gray paddles of the waterwheel. And all at once the low moaning sound started up again.

Melissa drew in her breath sharply. It was as if the ghostly sound were rising up over them, enveloping them. She clutched Jan's arm and said in a frightened gasp, "Listen!"

They stood like statues, straining their ears. The hollow, eerie sound was not coming from inside the old mill. It was coming from outside. It was coming from the old waterwheel below them!

They could only gape at one another in astonishment. "I don't believe it!" Audrey said in a quickly drawn breath. But even as she spoke, the breeze wafting off the pond became stronger, and the moaning sound through the old wheel rose to a shrill wail.

"Well, you better believe it," exclaimed Jan with a trembling laugh. "It's our ghost sounds all right."

Audrey craned her neck to stare down at the waterwheel. Her voice was still full of surprise when she said, "Then what we've been hearing is the wind blowing off the millpond and right through the old paddles of this wheel. And as it comes through the open window here, it fills the mill with a moaning and wailing kind of echo."

Jan nodded and said on a sudden thought, "It's a rare day when there's not some kind of breeze blowing off the millpond. Almost every time anybody comes by here and stops a while to listen, he's sure to hear it."

She paused and studied the open window. "I'll bet if this window had a pane of glass in it like in the old days, nobody would hear the sound."

They stopped talking. Looking at one another, they started giggling wildly. Imagine being frightened half to death by the wind blowing through an old waterwheel!

"Wait until Kevin and the kids hear about this," Audrey squealed with delight. "Will they ever be surprised!"

"I know one thing," Melissa vowed, "I'll never be afraid of ghosts again!"

She turned and gazed behind her at the gloomy interior of the old mill. No longer did its dusty walls and swaying cobwebs look grim and foreboding. Now that it had told its secret, the old mill seemed to have a sad and lonely air about it. Melissa felt almost sorry for the gloomy old building with its grim shadows and silently crumbling walls.

"You know what let's do," she said as a sudden inspiration came to her. "Let's pack a lunch and have a picnic here tomorrow. To keep the old mill company."

Audrey's eyes sparkled at the idea, and she began to discuss plans as they turned back from the window and made their way underneath the shadowy arms of the grain chutes, past the hopper, and around the white millstone.

The moaning sound rose up again as if it were following them, but no longer did it sound like the moaning of a ghost. Now it sounded like what it really was—the wind playing a grotesque tune through the warped boards of an old waterwheel.

147

Or, as Melissa liked to imagine, it sounded like the voice of the lonely old mill, bidding them good-bye and at the same time beckoning them to return.

Summer Girl

The rest of the week passed in a happy blur of activity. Melissa, Jan, and Audrey had their picnic at the gristmill, and after exploring the old building more thoroughly, even climbing up to the grain bins on the top floor, they spent the afternoon picking wild flowers along the millpond.

At first they found mostly pale bluets carpeting the moist bank; then Melissa found an unusual-looking flower half hidden under some dead leaves, like a jewel tucked away under brownleaf wrappings. She picked it and held it up to the sunlight. It was so delicate; it reminded her of a pretty figurine she had admired one time in a gift shop on Fifth Avenue.

149

"It looks like a tiny pink slipper," she cried as she examined the petals closely.

"That's how it got its name," Audrey explained. "It's called a lady's slipper."

Jan found a flower with clusters of tiny bell-like blossoms on its green stalk. "Here are bluebells," she told Melissa. She turned the flower upside down. "See, the blossoms really look like tiny blue bells."

Melissa laughed. "Hey, that's neat, calling flowers lady's slippers and bluebells!"

They looked around for as many different kinds of wild flowers as they could find. Audrey found a strange-looking yellow flower that grew up from the root of a tree, and told Melissa it was called a foxglove. They found Indian pipes, jack-in-the-pulpits, Dutchman's-breeches, buttercups, and solomon's-plumes. Melissa had never seen a dogtooth violet until she discovered one in the grass near where the horses were grazing.

When it was time to leave, the girls gathered their wild flowers together into bouquets and stuck them in the horses' bridles so that Shadow, Patches, and Silver Beauty looked quite festive as they trotted back along the forest trail.

When they crossed the road and came to the Triple J, they stopped by the bottom pasture to watch Princess and her colt. "Happy looks as if he's walking on stilts," Melissa observed as they watched the foal frisk about on his long, spindly legs.

"And wobbly stilts at that," Audrey agreed, laughing.

The rangy little colt's short, ragged tail waved at them as he trotted after Princess. When he turned to watch them, his curious brown eyes seemed much too big for his head, the same way his round body seemed much too large for his thin legs and dainty hooves. He was lopsided and awkward-looking now, but Jan told Melissa that by next summer he would be as beautiful and as surefooted as his mother. Even so, for all his awkwardness, Happy was the cutest thing Melissa had ever known.

Then came the day when Uncle Jeff and Ed decided it was time to halter the foal. As Melissa and Jan watched the two men come from the tack room with the small, foal-sized halter, Melissa asked, "Isn't Happy too young to be haltered?"

Jan shook her head. "Ed says a colt will be easier to handle later on if he's halter-broken early." She jumped down from the fence where they had been sitting. "Let's ask Dad if we can help put the halter on. After all, Happy's our foal."

Uncle Jeff consented and gave the girls the halter to hold out for Happy to see and to smell before it was slipped over his head. While Jan put the noseband over the colt's wriggling nose, Melissa slipped the headpiece over his head and fastened it under his jaw.

At first Happy was too curious to protest, but

when he sensed that the halter was on to stay, he tossed his head and stamped his hooves indignantly, leaping away from the girls and shaking his head furiously to try to remove the strange thing over his nose and ears. Princess nuzzled him, nickering reassuring sounds until at last he settled down.

"Does the halter hurt?" asked Melissa with concern.

Uncle Jeff shook his head. "No, it's just a nuisance to Happy, but he'll soon get used to it."

"We'll leave it on overnight," Ed said. "Tomorrow you girls can begin to lead him. He should be used to it by then."

So for the rest of the week Jan and Melissa took turns leading Happy around the bottom pasture. The little colt's training had begun.

All too soon the two weeks were over, and Melissa's vacation came to an end. On the day she left the Triple J she put on her pink shorts and white blouse and carefully packed the china horse among her other clothes in the suitcase so that it wouldn't break. Although it was Mama and Gran's gift, it would be hers too, for every time she would look at it on the table at home, it would remind her of Shadow and the Triple J.

The last thing Melissa did before the Mathews took her to Grayson's Store to meet the Fresh Air bus, was to slip out to the side yard and into the bottom pasture to say good-bye to the horses.

Shadow nickered and waved her golden tail as Melissa climbed over the fence. Princess trotted gracefully across the pasture, with Happy weaving awkwardly through the tall grass after her.

Melissa stroked Princess' nose. She threw her arms around Happy and gave him a big hug. Then she found the cube of sugar she had saved for Shadow and held it out on the palm of her hand, remembering the first time she had fed the beautiful sorrel.

Shadow took the sugar and nuzzled Melissa's shoulder with pleasing mumbles. Melissa ran her hand down the sorrel's muzzle and smoothed her forelock. She stood for several long minutes with her face pressed against Shadow's shoulder. The softness of the mare's trembling muzzle, the smell of her warm coat, the tossing forelock, the gentleness of her dark eyes—all so dear to Melissa—filled her with a warm happiness, and she knew she could never say good-bye forever to the beautiful sorrel.

After a while the Mathews and Ed joined her in the pasture. Ed smiled as he watched her standing by Shadow's side and put her thoughts into words. "I reckon nobody ever forgets the horse she first learned to ride."

"I know," Melissa murmured, and there was a catch in her voice because she knew that now it was time to leave.

"Good-bye," she said as she gave Shadow's muzzle a final pat and Happy another quick hug.

"I'll be back next summer to ride both of you."

"And next year it won't be just for two weeks," Uncle Jeff spoke up as if he were talking to the horses. "If she wants to, Missy will be spending the whole summer here at the Triple J. From now on she'll be our summer girl."

Jan slipped close to her side. "Isn't that neat, Missy!" she murmured. "And next summer we'll have even better times together because we'll have Happy to share."

With shining eyes Melissa looked at the smiling faces bent over her. Their summer girl! Now she knew that part of her would always belong here at the Triple J.

Tearful but smiling, her eyes met Jan's. Their hands came together, and the friendship bracelets caught and jingled.

Ruth Nulton Moore taught English and social studies in schools in Pennsylvania and Michigan. Along with writing poetry and stories for children's magazines, she has written nine juvenile novels. Several of her books have been translated into other languages and sell in England, Sweden, Finland, and Puerto Rico as well as in the United States and Canada.

Mrs. Moore lives in Bethlehem, Pennsylvania, with her husband, who is chairman of the department of accounting and law at Lehigh University. They have two sons, an attorney in Erie, Pennsylvania, and a student at West Virginia University.

A member of the Children's Authors and Illustrators of Philadelphia, Mrs. Moore lectures about the art of writing to students in public schools and colleges in her area.